WHO
CARES

WHO CARES

a memoir

Joyce E. Davies

GWADD
PUBLISHING

First published in Great Britain in 2022 by Gwadd Publishing

Copyright © 2022 by Joyce E. Davies
Formatted by The Amethyst Angel
Cover Image by Danny Muller

Author photo by Steve Davies, Classic Photography, Lincoln.

ISBN: 979-835-232-30-21

The moral right of the author has been asserted.

Names of people and places have been changed to protect identities.

First Edition

I dedicate my book to all the brave young people who find themselves in Care through no fault of their own.

ACKNOWLEDGEMENTS

My grateful thanks go to Michelle Gordon of The Amethyst Angel for her support and hard work in the publishing of this book.

Thanks to Annette Ecuyere for her patience and hard work during the time of writing of the manuscript.

My love and thanks go to my husband Glyn for his constant support during the time I worked with the girls and also when writing my book.

PROLOGUE

It had been a tiring journey, but at last we arrived. It was a rewarding sight as we gazed at lush pasture, cool mountains with sheep grazing, looking like so many fridge magnets as they grazed apparently motionless on the mountain side. We had arrived at the Outward Bound Activity Centre in Wales. In spite of the many "I didn't want to come anyway," and "aren't we there yet?" the girls looked with awe as the minibus drew up outside the low farmhouse building. "Ain't much doing here," mutterings were audible from the back seats.

As many of the girls, now tired after the long journey, reluctantly unplugged themselves from their Walkman's, we were greeted by a friendly and cheery man who introduced himself simply as Jack.

A voice piped up "Jack what? What do we call you? – Sir I expect."

"Jack will be just fine," he answered.

We unloaded baggage, in typical style, with some of the girls helping willingly while others just sat and stared into space in a nonchalant manner. When food was mentioned, straight away the general mood took a turn for the better. Jack then introduced us to the catering staff, a jolly group of women who would be looking after us during our stay. Quite a task as we consisted of twelve teenage girls and six staff.

"Hope the food's decent," Tracy muttered, "Hope it ain't this vegetable rubbish." Tracy had a particular aversion to eating anything wholesome. However, the catering staff were experienced in catering for teenagers, and although we staff might have to "grin and eat it" the girls would be well fed on burgers, sausages, chips and the like, with plenty of fruit and salads for those who wanted them.

We were ushered into a large refectory where tables were laid out attractively with pretty mats and a small vase of fresh flowers on each one. It was too much for any of the girls to make a positive comment, but we adults exclaimed at the attractiveness and welcome of the room. The girls managed to seat themselves with the minimum of fuss, as they jostled into a seat with their special friends, or as in the case of Sian, sitting by herself hoping one of the others would sit next to her. I felt sad for her as she was at the bottom of the pecking order in this group. The prettier and brighter girls were definitely at the top, with one or two of the clever ones sometimes marginalized.

This trip was a treat for the girls who had just completed their GCSE's. Many of them had never had a holiday so opted to come, whereas others had chosen to remain at the school, and would be taken out for treats such as the zoo or the swimming pool. Although it had been their choice, we knew that the inevitable would happen and we would be faced with "I wish I'd stayed in England" or "I wish I'd gone on the treats."

After tea, a walk was suggested and after the usual arguments we managed to get everyone to agree. Jack accompanied us and led us through a big field, accompanied by shrieks from some of the girls who could not accept the fact that the sheep droppings covering the area were the natural progression of the animals feeding. No animals were in evidence at the time.

We came to a clearing where a waterfall presented itself, gushing and foaming. We all shed our shoes and socks and paddled in the fresh icy water that streamed down from the hills. "Good 'ere ain't it?" said Bev with nods of agreement from the other girls. To be too enthusiastic would not have been 'cool,' it wouldn't do to show that they were enjoying themselves. It was a warm evening, but the shadows casting themselves across the water made it feel chilly. With much argument and objections from the girls as usual, who always fought against any discipline metered out to them, even if it was for their own good, a unanimous decision was made by staff and girls to return to the centre. At the mention of supper the girls hurried each other with enthusiastic sounds such as "last one in is a sissy."

After supper the girls settled down quietly chatting and making plans for the following day. Jack would be driving us to the pony trekking centre where ponies had been booked for us. Then into the silence came a loud voice. "I won't be coming to the horse thing as its me mum's birfday day after tomorrer and I got to get her a card and post it first class." Trust Bev to upset the applecart. Looking over at me who happened to be sitting opposite her she asked "You'll come with me Miss won't yer?" I agreed, thinking that there must be a post office in the village and we could easily catch up with the others.

The care staff spent time sorting out the girls' accommodation, with of course the usual arguments about who would share with whom, until the girls seemed settled. The staff had sorted out their accommodation previously.

I drifted off to sleep quite quickly as it had been a long day when I woke to hear a shout, and I thought 'am I dreaming or what?' Then Elli, who was sharing my room shouted, "Up we get, Sian is on the run again." This is what the staff had feared. There had been the question of whether or not Sian would be allowed to come on this trip, but as her behaviour had improved of late, and she was very keen to come, having been born in Wales 16 years previously, we had been persuaded to include her.

We struggled into jeans and jerseys and arrived at the

main house to find that Jack had organized a search and this was going ahead in an orderly manner. He gave each of us a torch with instructions to spread out. This being an isolated spot, with a reservoir a quarter of a mile away we feared for the safety of this unstable and vulnerable girl. We spread out, everyone calling in varying tones of encouragement or exasperation.

This was not a new phenomenon for us, as Sian was classified as one of the girls who occasionally 'went on the run'. The normal pattern was for her to 'run' very early in the morning and as the bus and train stations were very near to the school in the London area, she could disappear to various places, and we knew where to look. These places included the homes of Social workers, care staff or a friend she knew she could trust.

Our Sian had a strong sense of self-preservation and would not put herself knowingly in an acutely dangerous position. Eventually Jack went back to the hostel and returned to tell us that in fact Sian was sitting in the kitchen sipping a mug of cocoa with the catering staff members clustered around her making sure she was alright. I wanted to wipe the smug look off her face, but instead said. "Sian, we are all so glad that you are okay. You had us all so worried." She turned away to hide a triumphant look.

The anger I felt immediately melted away as I thought of the life she had lived before being placed in care. One without love or care, only sexual and verbal abuse and beatings. I went up and gave her a big hug. We had a special relationship as I too am Welsh, born and bred as was she.

I woke quite early to sunshine and a piebald sky patched with clouds. The sun was strong enough to give the promise of a fine day to come.

All appeared quiet after the previous night and with breakfast over, Bev and I planned the day. Looking at the local map we saw that the village Post Office was just a short walk away. The catering staff were clearing away and one of them leaned over the map and said "It's no good you going to the Post Office, bach, it's closed for repairs."

Bev was alarmed. "We got to get the card and send it anyway," she insisted as if by magic a ready stamped card and a post office would materialise. "Don't worry we'll get a card somewhere" I assured her with a confidence I was far from feeling. We were assured that the nearest open Post Office was in a nearby village, quite accessible if we were prepared to walk. We were here on an outward bound holiday so that should be fine. Jack appeared and told us that the journey would be half a mile. "Was it as the crow flies, or what?" I asked myself.

We set off with me clutching the map directions that had been put together by Mary, a member of staff at the hostel. I couldn't help but muse on the fact that here was a 15 year old child, whose parents had abused and virtually disowned her only agreeing, after a struggle with Social Workers, to have her home even for one night, moving heaven and earth to see that her Mum had a birthday card on time. The love these children seemed to have for their Mums and Dads was beyond belief.

The sun had come up and we walked along the path with Bev chatting away about this and that. One or two people passed us who appeared to be locals and greeted us with a friendly "Bore Da," aimed mainly at Bev who was a very pretty girl and obviously charmed with the Welsh countryside, as she had a look on her face which said 'all this is wonderful', as she surveyed the scene before her. "I ain't been to the country before," she confided.

We plodded on, stopping occasionally to sip water from the bottles we were carrying. Eventually we spotted a sign that announced that a Post Office was in the vicinity. At last I thought, and even though I had enjoyed the walk in the fresh country air, I had suffered misgivings on the way, as these girls were sometimes unpredictable and would run off if provoked in any way that they considered a threat.

On entering the Post Office we were again greeted with a cheery "Bore Da." Spotting that we were obviously visitors, the woman then spoke English with a very strong Welsh accent that we both found difficult to understand. However, it was soon established that we were on a mission for a birthday card with Mum on it and it had to go today, as Bev made all this clear in her rather loud cockney accent. We were in luck, they had a number of cards, all suitable. One was duly chosen, written, stamped and posted carefully.

As we made our way back to the hostel I just hoped that the next few days of the holiday would be less eventful, that the girls would settle down in their new environment and there would be no more 'midnight flights'. This proved to be the case as we all returned to school in one piece, both tired and happy after a wonderful holiday.

PART ONE

CHAPTER ONE

I entered the large, impressive grounds with much trepidation. All was quiet; the manicured lawns and well-kept borders suggested organised calm! The small board on the gatepost informed the visitor that indeed this was RAVENSCOURT. No other information was provided as to what the establishment was, private house or school. I knew it was a school, newly opened after some years of closure, to be run as a CHE school, a community home with education for girls aged 13 – 18 with social needs and behavioural problems brought on by physical and/or sexual abuse etc.

I had researched the history of the building. The present house dated back to around 1600 when it had been built on an estate, which dated back to 1286. The house had changed hands many times since then. Much refurbishment had taken place at great expense to each of the owners. But eventually it fell into disrepair. Now somewhat restored, it looked from the outside, like the grand affluent residence it once was.

The inside I was soon to learn had been altered and adjusted to fit into a life which consisted of living accommodation for 15 girls.

The mansion consisted of five floors. The ground floor contained the classrooms and was known as "School", plus the room that had been fashioned as the Chapel, looking splendid with thick red carpeting and all the trappings of a beautiful chapel where the Sisters could pray and meditate and where Mass could be celebrated. The first and second floors consisted of a large unit which housed the bedrooms and living areas of the girls and the senior care staff who were on shifts so that there would be staff to care for the girls at all times. The third floor housed the study of Sister Mary Head of Ravenscourt, also the office of the School Secretary Janette and her assistant Wendy. The fourth floor housed various rooms which housed bedrooms for members of care staff who "slept in." This floor also revealed what the girls would come to call "the padded room" which had been used when the building had previously been run as a Reform School. The walls were thickly padded with foam, hence the name.

I entered the front door which led into a large area with an impressive staircase carpeted in red. The area looking too grand to contain any school activities I had ever seen! "Hi," a friendly voice called, which I recognised as Janet's, who had been at the extensive interview procedure we had all been subject to, which had taken place away from site. It was good to hear her voice as it gave me confidence that I had done the right thing to give up a well-paid job in a sixth form college to branch out into, what I believed, to be working in a more caring situation than previously.

I had enjoyed teaching the bright young people although the classes had been large, yet I often felt that I just seemed to the students to be someone who had just appeared from a filing cabinet and was not a person in my own right. Bright as most of the students were, there were many problems and a teacher had to be strong to cope with these teenagers, whatever their intelligence and background. I would have to see what this previous experience of teenagers had done to prepare me for the challenge to come.

"The teachers staff room is just down this corridor" said Janet "most of us are here already." On entering the quite small room I saw that five members of the newly-formed teaching staff had gathered. We were all teaching different subjects, with Sister Angela as the Head of Education. They were a friendly bunch and I had already met most of them at the interviews. I felt at home immediately. We were all in the same boat, all newcomers to this type of work, apart from Janet who had worked in this type of environment previously.

It would be a learning curve for most of us. There was to be an induction two days before the students were expected. I was surprised to see that all the teaching staff were woman of varying ages. The door opened and Sister Mary entered the room. She welcomed us all and started our induction. There were rules and regulations to be followed as in any organisation. We were then shown our classrooms.

My classroom was a light and airy one at the front of the building overlooking the extensive lawns. 'That's a good start,' I thought to myself as I began to sort myself out. With my lesson plans in order, I wondered nervously whether they would have to be drastically adjusted or even altered to fit in with the kind of girl we were expecting.

The community home was being led by a group of Roman Catholic Sisters of the Order of St Teresa; led by Sister Mary. As it turned out, she was the one who ruled the school with a rod of iron, but became highly respected and even loved by us all. The Head of Education was Sister Angela, a nun in her thirties who appeared highly efficient and friendly. However there was a glint in her eye which seemed to be a challenge as if to say "Don't mess with me."

This was certainly going to be a completely new experience for me. Working for nuns was the last thing I wanted if the truth was known. The interviews had been held in Bristol in a school which had already been run by this organization of nuns and they were now moving on to run Ravenscourt, which needed a complete reorganization after being run as an approved school for girls, but closed owing to, "circumstances beyond the control of the original organization." During the extensive interviews, although the Sisters were very pleasant and non-threatening, it had felt like being back at school. I had heard many tales of nuns who had been both quietly angry and downright nasty in their dealings with the "outside world" so we will see! With hindsight it would appear that I was more worried about my relationship with the nuns than with possibly disruptive teenage girls with personal and social problems.

The first day of term dawned, and to say that I was nervous was an under-statement. We were expected to attend assembly so all the teachers lined up to enter the hall which was a very large room with heavy oak panelling on the walls and worn but expensive oak parquet flooring. I mused on the fact that this seemed to have been the ballroom in the original house.

I was pleased to see the other teachers were also nervous. The Head was already in the hall and the girls had all arrived accompanied by their care workers. We all sat in a large circle. As I glanced around at the girls I saw that they were all busily weighing up their new teachers, one or two with actual distrust it seemed. Well, it was up to us to make school an interesting place for them, some of whom, we had been told had suffered bad experiences at school. The Assembly began with a prayer by Sister Mary, and a Bible verse was read by one of the nuns. There were five nuns altogether, in positions of Care worker or House mother. A short talk followed, with various topics used, but these Assemblies set the tone for the day, and indeed the calming influence seemed to work as the girls filed out to their classes in an orderly manner.

I entered my classroom and was met by blank stares from most of the girls. "Not a good start," I thought, but as there were only six girls in my class I would have no problem – or would I? I introduced myself and wrote the date on the board.

"We know the date, Miss," said one bright spark looking about 10 years old, but must have been at least thirteen. She was a tiny girl with a mop of curls and a pretty face which was spoilt by a frown. I smiled and asked her name.

"My name's Janine, Miss," she replied in a somewhat sulky manner. This one was going to be a challenge all right.

They were an assorted bunch, pretty and plain. I took the register and handed out text books, pens and paper and the lesson began. They each worked or not their own pace, and as I was used mainly to highly motivated students I found it hard going, as I tried to work "with them" and not "against them." I had taken this job and I was jolly well going to make it work.

At the forefront of my mind I kept telling myself that these girls had suffered both emotionally and physically and deserved understanding and help and I was here to give it. I was later to learn just how much emotional, physical and sexual abuse all of these girls had suffered in their own way. The day wore on and tired, but satisfied that things had gone reasonably well, the day came to an end.

As the weeks went by we all settled down and a good working relationship developed between girls, care staff and teachers. As well as the core curriculum, the subjects taught were Cookery, Art, History, and Business Studies.

On my second day I entered the classroom to find the girls, all six of them sitting quietly behind their desks, waiting with what I thought was expectancy for the lesson to begin. Then a slight disruption started as two of the girls sitting in the middle of a row started to giggle as they passed a sheet of paper quickly to whoever would become involved. They then began the sniffing process as a small container of glue was passed around. It all happened so quickly. I acted spontaneously as I grabbed the glue, threw it on the top of a handy cupboard and snatched the paper which I ripped up. I managed to keep quite calm as I carried out this task. They were rendered speechless so I felt something had been achieved! Did they think I was so green as not to recognise glue sniffing? These girls were not much different to those I had taught previously, although they were more overt in their bad behaviour. I decided not to report this incident, but when the opportunity arose I would ask permission to give a talk on the dangers of drug abuse, and where it could lead.

Most teachers use a broad range of skills and techniques, which includes their knowledge, experience, relationships, thoughts and activities, classed as personal, interpersonal, organisational and community sources. The most commonly used strategies such as 'try to keep things in perspective', 'try to avoid confrontation' and 'relax after work' are of great importance.

On the whole the girls liked school for the discipline and order that it brought to their lives. All seemed fairly calm, but I felt that there was always something simmering in the background. Staff support is so important in this work. So apart from the weekly staff meeting with the Head, there was much support within the teaching group as we shared problems and sought advice from each other, especially when discussing difficulties which were threatening to become major pressure, as we shared coping actions.

We evolved into a close caring group where we were able to release feelings of tension, anxiety, frustration and sometimes anger. In my experience, teaching in a care situation differs greatly from secondary school main stream education, where members of staff are very rarely encouraged to share problems and where all staff appear highly motivated, highly efficient and capable, not showing any weaknesses and often not appearing to have any.

I was slowly getting to know the girls, and over the weeks, several new ones were joining us, being referred to the school to by their local authority, which was mainly Inner London. It appeared that the school was getting a good reputation and I felt pleased that I had decided to move to this work.

One morning I came into the classroom to find a new girl seated at the front desk. She looked about 16 and she eyed me with hostility. I asked her name, "Dana" she replied, followed by "You are a rotten teacher and I'm not working for you."

"You don't know what I'm like," I replied, as she promptly lifted up her plump little legs and placed them on the desk. Fearing a confrontation I replied "Okay." and carried on working with the others. I gave out books and started to write on the board. The other girls simply ignored her.

We were informed that several new girls would be joining us in the next few weeks and months and I hoped that there would not be any more Dana's. Although the staff had open access to the personal files of each girl and some teachers liked to read them in preparation for what might be to come, I had decided not to, preferring to form my opinion of the girl from the day she appeared and not to have my opinion of her "coloured" by her previous actions, however bad.

As time went by and we gained their trust, the girls would share "in confidence" what they had done. Many of them had been put in care for their own safety from abuse. I got used to their stories, many passed on by members of teaching or care staff who had read their files relating to physical and mental abuse alongside horrendous tales of sexual abuse of sisters such as Stacy and Natalie who had both been abused by their father and teenage brother, apparently with the complete knowledge of their mother. Many girls had been violent as we heard stories of arson where one girl had set fire to her school. She actually informed me of this proudly one day. GBH and ABH were common, as were the taking of vehicles and driving away.

I had been carrying on with my class which met for three lessons a week, ignoring Dana sitting at the front. One day she put her legs down and informed me, "I'm going to work for you now, Miss."

"Good" I said, and handed her a work sheet. She did in fact work for me, and one day invited me for tea at her unit, which cemented our relationship and from then on she worked diligently for me, passing the exams set before her. She even kept in touch with me when she left school a couple of years later and I was able to follow her progress through a number of years.

CHAPTER TWO

School continued at a steady pace, of course as was to be expected there were minor problems with the girls, but on the whole things were much as I had expected. Major problems were to arise however, as one morning during lessons a loud crash was heard followed by breaking glass which appeared to be coming from the classroom next door. A number of the girls jumped up and made for the door, I managed with difficulty to persuade them to return to their seats as I promised to investigate. "You can be in charge while I investigate," I told Miriam who was a sensible member of the class and took any responsibilities she was handed with great solemnity. I knew the others would respect a strong member of their peer group. She strutted importantly to the front of the class. "Don't worry, Miss, I'll see they behave," she informed me as I disappeared through the door.

The sight as I entered the classroom was disconcerting

to say the least. One of the large windows was shattered, with glass everywhere and most of the girls in the class of six were just standing around silently, except for the culprit who had broken the window. She was standing near the window with a smug look! My first thought was that no one appeared to be hurt which was a miracle considering the amount of glass on the floor. Diane, for that was her name as I later discerned, had disagreed with the teacher and decided she had had enough, and school was a waste of time anyway. She had picked up the nearest chair which was a lightweight metal one and thrown it through the large plate glass window onto the lawn below. I was amazed at her strength. The teacher in charge was experienced, so why had it happened? I knew none of us had heard the last of this, as it was the policy of the school that a Community meeting would be held in the hall with all staff and students expected to attend when a major problem had occurred, and indeed this was 'major'.

Returning to the classroom I was surprised to find the girls engrossed in their work. "Thank you, Miriam" I said as she returned to her seat and carried on as if nothing unusual had happened. With a shock I realised that what had been unexpected and a "first" for me was in fact for them a happening they had encountered possibly many times before.

The Community meeting took place the following morning. I was very nervous, not knowing if I was expected to contribute. None of the teaching staff were prepared, but it appeared that most of the talking was done by the Care staff who knew these girls better than us as they saw them 24/7. I found this event unsettling as the teacher concerned had to set the case before us. She did not appear to know what exactly had sparked off this anger from the girl. Sister Mary was in charge and asked the culprit "Well Diane what have you got to say for yourself?"

Diane mumbled and said "I don't know, she just made me angry." Following discussion she was told she would be given another chance, and should anything like that happen again it would be taken further and she might be sent to a secure unit in another part of the country. This was my first experience of a Community meeting and I was surprised to find myself quite shaken by it. However, it was the first of many I was to experience in the eight years I spent in this school. So, I got used to knowing when to speak out and when to remain silent.

The staff had been informed that we would be expecting new girls to join us, and we should be prepared for this. New students joining an established group could sometimes cause a few problems. Not that one could call the present girls 'an established group'. They seemed to get on well with one another when they were together, although there did not appear to be any couplings. Each girl was an individual, more or less keeping to themselves as if saying "I am not going to let my guard down, No way!" They had obviously been badly let down in the past and were taking no chances.

They were a mixed bunch which made teaching them more interesting. Mostly white, and three girls of African origin. Their behaviour in class was good and they paid attention. They had difficulties communicating in group work, so I had to introduce this to them slowly.

So the first term went on. As in all teaching situations there were minor disturbances, but the girls carried on working at the set task for the most part. I began to feel more relaxed and enjoyed the new challenge.

During our weekly staff meetings it appeared that we were all settling into our new positions teaching our various subjects, although I did pick up that some of us had higher and different expectations of the students. This probably depended on our age and previous teaching experience. The Head of school, Sister Angela, informed us that two new girls would be joining us during the next two weeks and we should be prepared for this.

I observed with interest the effect the nuns had on the girls. Apart from Sister Angela, the other four nuns of the Order were in caring positions. The girls seemed to hold the nuns in great esteem. Perhaps it was the wimple. I think there was a slight fear present as if they thought the nuns had special powers! Each girl had a Key worker on site and an outside Social worker who worked closely with the parents/guardian of the child. Group meetings were held at intervals, when the parents/guardians, Key worker, Social worker and Teacher were present.

The day came when the first of the two expected new

girls appeared. We were all surprised. Dawn looked like a model. In spite of her being very modestly and quite shabbily dressed she had a beautiful face, long blond hair and a bearing that carried these off. She was gorgeous and she knew it. We were all introduced to her in Assembly. When spoken to she looked down modestly but I could see a glint in her eye which informed the rest of us, "I'm not all I seem." When she came to my classes she behaved well, worked constantly, and in a short time became head of the pecking order. It seemed everyone wanted to be her friend.

Sian was the next girl to join us. Her surname was Evans so I wondered if she had any Welsh connections. Being Welsh myself, having lived in England for 30 years I was always on the lookout for a Welsh connection with people, however tenuous. Sian did not hesitate to inform me that she was in fact Welsh, originally from the valleys. She picked up my accent straight away. She had a slight Welsh accent and seemed to gravitate towards me from the first. She settled in alright but was always bottom of the pecking order. She was a quiet girl and so encouraged the bullies in the group to take advantage of her. There was never any overt bullying, the girls were too clever for that.

Most of the girls were bright, but suffered from low self-esteem and poor self-image, rarely having had any encouragement or praise in their lives so far. We teachers did our best to praise and encourage any good work being done but were careful not to overdo it and sound patronising.

Now that the numbers were increasing, a tutor system had been introduced in the school. Each teacher would be allocated one to three girls depending on the numbers in school. The tutor would be responsible for the well-being, school attendance, behaviour, homework and needs of each girl during the school day. This system proved very valuable both to the girl and the teacher. We were allowed to take them off site for a short time to a café or to the local Library following a very strict regime. It was not encouraged, but allowed under special circumstances such as the Tutor group having a treat. The first time I took three girls to a MacDonald's which I found great fun but noticed the small group dynamics which I had not expected. Very quietly they asked one another who was going to pay for the meal! In my book if you invite someone for a meal it means you pay but not so in their book. My heart went out to them. They solved the problem very cleverly. "Who is going to pay, Miss, is it you or are you going to claim back in expenses?" whispered the bravest member of the little group. "I am of course" I replied, "I never invite anyone out for a meal if I don't intend to pay." They were happy with this, and it boded well for the further meals and outings which I took them on.

Another advantage from the teacher's point of view, was being invited by the girls, to visit their home environment two floors above. There was a warm welcome from the Housemother, a middle-aged homely woman with vast experience of teenage girls, especially those with problems of the sort she was now encountering. My first invitation was from Sian who was one of my "tutees." She made me a cup of tea and provided a biscuit. It was obviously a new situation for her to be in, looking after and catering for a "grownup" and she revelled in it. She then invited me into her bedroom which was neat and tidy.

Each girl had a room to herself, which although small, was more than adequate. It contained a small washbasin as the bathroom was shared. After the niceties of me saying, "what a lovely room, you do keep it neat and tidy," and her reply "Thanks, Miss," I was very surprised at the next chain of events.

"Because you're Welsh I can talk to you, Miss." I was very pleased that she felt safe enough to confide in me, but wondered what was to come, yet not prepared for what followed. "Do you know why I am in care, Miss?" she said tentatively.

I was able to reply honestly. "No, I never read the file of any girl." Leaving it at that. Sian then confided in me, that when she was a small girl living in Wales "in a long row of houses that all looked the same" her grandfather abused her, taking every opportunity when her parents were out at work, which seemed a lot of the time, as they were hard -up and needed to work. I tried to hide my horror, Sian did not notice as she proceeded with her story. "Not only that, Grandpa used to call in the old man next door." I wanted to ask questions, but my throat seemed to be closing up. She carried on for a little longer, but it failed to sink in as I was so shocked. It was probably naïve of me, I had heard of this sort of thing but had never come against it face to face. I flattered myself that I was street-wise, as I had spent a number of years drugs counselling, but this shook me rigid, although It did prepare me for the stories I heard from other girls in the future.

Sian sensed my feelings as she looked intently into my face. "I'm so sorry Sian," I said, and put my hand out. As a teacher I know it is not admissible to have physical contact with the children in your care. I was soon to learn however, that working in this environment, rules get thrown out of the window. It is a caring situation after all! Suddenly Sian moved close to me. We held hands in silence. Nothing more was said but this particular afternoon cemented a relationship between us.

Numbers grew as local authorities referred girls mainly from Inner London areas, which meant we were running short of rooms. Contained within the vast grounds there was an annexe containing living accommodation, bedrooms, bathrooms etc. Apparently this accommodation had been used previously when the site had been a reform school for girls. Refurbishment was carried out and the building housed the extra girls. These girls integrated very well and extra care staff was drafted in. All members of care staff at that time were qualified and/or experienced, and the 'houses' as the units were now called settled down. School went on as usual and the newcomers seemed to settle in class. It meant extra work for the teachers, but this had been expected and catered for with the classrooms being large and easily able to contain the extra chairs and desks that were brought in.

On the surface all seemed calm. The weeks went by and the people of the small town accepted the girls, as they saw them out and about usually accompanied by a member of Care staff or a Teacher. Most of the girls in spite of their past problems, some of which were truly horrific, and not having highly developed social skills, managed to convey a friendliness with a smile and a hello when spoken to briefly.

It was during this time that the Brixton riots were taking place. Starting in April 1981 they were the first serious riots of the 20th century in England. These were sparked by antagonism between black youths and the police, as rioting, looting and arson took place. At the time, The Guardian newspaper reported that the tension between the police and youths led to Brixton being set aflame. 1985 saw the second major riot that the area had witnessed in the space of four years.

Brixton had been 'home' to some of our girls, who had been brought up there. They took these riots in their stride, and being very young they did not know the full background story, therefore they blamed the police.

Instead of being just a story, these events took a serious turn for us at Ravenscourt. The TV and newspapers of the time reported that a gang of black youths had attacked a white girl and left her in an alley where she had been badly beaten. Although this beating was not directly connected to the riots, it happened at the same time.

It had been reported that this beating had been carried out by a gang of youths, but what they omitted to say was that one of the gang of youths was a girl.

A new girl of African origin arrived suddenly at Ravenscourt. This was unusual as we were normally informed in advance of any new girls joining us. We were told that she was in fact one of the gang involved in the Brixton beating of a white girl. This was difficult to believe as she was a quiet, tiny unassuming girl aged 13 who only stayed with us for a short time, before being moved into Care elsewhere. One never knew what to expect when working in a job such as ours, we had to be prepared for all eventualities.

One day a member of care staff and four girls paid a visit to town. New clothes were needed so off they went. A couple of hours later all returned and the girls seemed high with some sort of hidden excitement. New clothes, I thought. However, when they returned home, the reason for this was found to be the fact that hidden under their coats they each had a garment, stolen from a local chain store. It was also discovered that Rena had a large piece of cheese in her pocket. Stilton with wine! No ordinary mousetrap cheese for Rena. We had to laugh, not in front of the girls of course. This was the sort of behaviour all children got up to. My own son at the age of about 8 confessed to me once that David and Peter, two of his mates had "stolen sweets from the local shop." I was cross about such a thing as I said to him "I hope you didn't steal anything." "Of course not," he replied "I was just the lookout!"

The girls were marched back to the relevant shops where they apologised profusely, apparently putting on an act of true repentance! They were clever actors these girls. When out of sight of the shops they collapsed in a heap shrieking with laughter. The staff had been very forgiving and nothing more was to be said about the matter. During the eight years I had worked at Ravenscourt there had been many occasions when the press could have got hold of a juicy tale or two, but thankfully it never happened. Staff never discussed any of the troubles when we were outside the school, as we tried to keep a fairly low profile, just getting on with the job in hand to the best of our ability.

Christmas was fast approaching and we wondered what we could do in school to make it interesting. The Sisters wanted a Nativity play, so we all came up with ideas to make it a success. We need not have worried too much as when the time came, gifts were sent in from outside. The highlight was free tickets for all girls and several staff to a local pantomime. Richmond Theatre was putting on the pantomime Cinderella. Anita Dobson was playing the prince. "She's on telly" the girls chorused when they heard the news. This was the 80s and Anita Dobson was high profile at the time.

The outing was a big success, the only blip was when the ice-cream girl came round calling: "Free ice-creams for the Ravenscourt girls." On hearing this they put their heads down as if they had something to hide. I doubt if anyone listening would even know that the school mentioned was a school for girls with problems of the sort they had suffered. The outing was enjoyed by all and was the first of many free seats at the theatre and BBC filmings the school was given over the years.

There was only one rule laid down when accompanying students to such outings. A member of staff must accompany a girl at all times. Any drifting away from the group was not permitted, and if not looked out for this was likely to happen. This was not allowed, whether it was for the toilet or any other reason. This could be hard on the girls and also stressful for staff who had to be on watch the whole time, but rules were rules, and that was that.

Christmas came and went. It had been a fun time for staff and girls. The nativity play had been arranged by Sister Angela with the girls playing all the parts and Sister Angela playing her guitar which she did very successfully. There had been an exchange of cards and I was very touched when a number of girls presented me with a card.

CHAPTER THREE

The new term began and we all settled into routine. What sort of year could we look forward to I wondered. We were all a lot busier now that there were 26 girls in the school, all with their individual needs.

One day I noticed cuts on the arms of two girls. Tara tried to hide hers by pulling down her sleeves, while Natalie seems to flout hers as she pushed hers up. The other girls in the class ignored the body language of the two; they had probably encountered it many times previously. Maybe even cut themselves at some time? I was familiar with this kind of teenage self-punishment, but had not encountered it first-hand. As this kind of behaviour was not in a teacher's remit I decided to ignore it, thinking that later I would have a word with the relevant key-workers, who would probably be able to fill me on at least some of the details. It can be hard to understand why people cut themselves on purpose. Cutting can be a way of trying to cope with the pain of strong emotions, intense pressure or upsetting relationship problems. They may be dealing with feelings that seem too difficult to bear or bad situations they believe they cannot change. Also their coping skills may be overpowered by emotions that are too intense and cutting may be an attempt to relieve that extreme tension. It might feel to them like being in control after living through abuse or violence.

Time went on without any major happenings, with the girls settled into the home and school routine and on the whole their attitude and behaviour good. What I found unusual was how the relationship between pupils and teachers progressed. Morning assembly was well organised. Teachers were the first to arrive, followed by the girls and their key workers in orderly procession. I noticed after a while, the girls instead of staring straight ahead one or two of them seemed to be scanning the faces of the teachers, and instead of sitting together or with their key workers, they began to sit near or next to some of the teachers. Sian came to sit next to me and linked arms. I smiled at her encouragingly. "Morning Sian," I said and was rewarded by a shy smile.

One Monday morning we were greeted with the news that Sian had "jumped" out of an upstairs window. The news was delivered with such calm that we realised she had not been injured or worse. My heart missed a beat. It didn't bear thinking about. "She's OK" said Diane, the Care worker. How anyone could be OK after falling from a window I couldn't think! We were taken to inspect the window, which considering the height of the building, a relatively low one. She had fallen onto a small patch of lawn.

"Good thing she's fat," said Diane. Hardly a kind thing to say under the circumstances. Sian had been taken to A&E, where after extensive examination had been pronounced physically fit, no bones broken, but mentally traumatised from the 'fall.' A couple of days rest was recommended. "The fact that she is quite plump saved the day," announced the doctor. Sian's Social worker was sent for, and a decision agreed that no further action was to be taken. Of course, knowing her background, the question still remained 'Did she jump or did she fall?'

For the next couple of days I pondered for a way I could help Sian. She was a Welsh speaker, and was disappointed that Welsh was not my first language, so we could not converse in her chosen language. I had an idea. June a good friend of mine, also a teacher locally and a fluent Welsh speaker might be able to help. I contacted her that evening. As I knew she would, she said she would be delighted to help. "I could come one evening a week to teach Sian Welsh" she said. I would have to clear it with the Head of school, Sister Angela who readily agreed. I put the idea to Sian who seemed to have recovered completely from her fall, as everyone decided to call it, "That would be nice, Miss" she said, appearing to be cool about the proposition, but I could tell by her body language that she was delighted, as she clasped her hands together in excitement, as we planned when the first lesson would take place.

She and June took to each other from the first meeting, and the Welsh lessons became a regular Tuesday evening event that was looked forward to. Sian came to trust my friend and shared many of her problems with her, as she had with me but not in such great depth. It was obvious that Sian saw the Welsh lessons as very important, but the most important thing was that someone had gone out of their way to arrange something purely for her, and this gave her confidence and a sense of worth that she was important enough for anyone to do this.

Our weekly teaching staff meetings confirmed that on the whole 'school' was quite successful. All teachers agreed that the girls were motivated so long as we were able to hold their interest, which wasn't always easy. They worked at their lessons and questions were asked as to when we could work towards achieving qualifications for them. It was also decided at this meeting that we would plan outside educational visits: The Science Museum, the V&A, and possibly the National Gallery in London. Taking no more than six to eight girls at a time, with three or four teachers accompanying them.

Arrangements were made for a trip to the Science Museum for eight of the girls and three teachers. We were dropped off at the local station by our mini-bus. The train took us to south Kensington station, and after a short walk we would arrive at our destination. We were all looking forward to the day. There was the inevitable, "I don't feel like going," and "what are we going for?" This was expected and ignored for the most part by the accompanying adults.

As we were travelling out of peak hours the train was relatively empty, except for two middle-aged ladies, who were all dressed up and looking forward to spending a day up in town, as we suburbians called the city of London. The girls sat in twos at one side of the aisle, while we teachers sat the other side, keeping a watchful eye on what was going on. The girls were chatting excitedly among themselves the way teenagers do. Then one of the ladies got up from her seat, went over to the girls, and leaning menacingly over them said "Be quiet, why have you girls got to make so much noise, when some of us are enjoying a quiet day out?" I suddenly realised how protective I had become over the girls. I went over; I don't think she had noticed that they were accompanied by adults. I realised I had become angry on their behalf. I kept my cool. "Excuse me," I said, "I am one of the teachers of these girls and if their behaviour had been anything but acceptable we certainly would have done something about it." I noticed her friend cringing in her seat. I appeared from her body language that she thought her friend something of a bully. She had probably herself been subject to the bullying at one time or another. The challenger said nothing more, and returned to her seat. All of a sudden the girls began clapping me. Then I did lose my cool. "Be quiet" I shouted, and as they had never before heard me raise my voice they did just that. The rest of the journey to West Kensington was uneventful, but I think the two ladies were glad to see us out of the way. The day was enjoyed, the girls busy writing in the notebooks that had been provided. The mini-bus picked up a tired, but satisfied group at the station. The first Educational outing had been successful. However, the confrontation with the two ladies in the train remained a talking point as the girls rushed up to the care staff relating the tale how Miss had stood up to the bossy lady. Something I preferred to forget.

One morning all was peaceful in class as each girl worked at her own pace. The windows of my classroom were long and wide and a good view of the extensive lawns was to be had by all who cared to look. There was normally nothing to be seen. Hardly any activity in the small visitor's car park. There were very few visitors to Ravenscourt. I then heard some activity in the group followed by "Who's she?", "Look at that car!", "What's she doing here?"

Looking up, I beheld an unusual sight. A slim glamorous blond in a powder-blue trouser suit, with a perfectly sculpted hairdo, was stepping out of what I later found out to be a silver Porsche. What was she doing here indeed? Like something out of a film set, no wonder the girls were impressed, as indeed was I. By now most of them had risen from their seats. We all gawped in amazement, before I came to my senses and told the girls to sit down, promising I would find out later who she was and what she wanted? As indeed I did. Discussion took place in the staffroom at lunchtime. Sisters Mary and Angela filled us in. Her name was Mary-Ann, she was looking for voluntary work and had always wanted to work with 'under-privileged' girls. The teachers exchanged glances. 'Poor little rich girl' I unkindly thought. She was in her late twenties, had no teaching or care qualifications In spite of this, the Sisters were completely captivated and with no further consultation she was in! Starting the following week on a one day weekly basis to begin with. As it happens it was a month before she began work due to Police checks etc. "I'm sure she will fit in well," the Head assured us. 'They have no idea of how the real world works,' I thought. As only qualified staff were taken on we were surprised at how the rules were now being bent to fit in with this obviously wealthy individual.

As we later found out Mary-Ann lived with a much older boy-friend, and lived in a posh house in a well-known gated estate. The Porsche was a second car, the first, a 'grown-up' car, was a Rolls-Royce. Well, we'll see I thought, not feeling at all optimistic at the thought of her fitting in with the teachers in the first instance, as we were told by the Head, "I know I can rely on my teachers to guide and help her."

'Saints Days' were of vital importance in the lives of the sisters, each sister having their special day during which a Saint is celebrated, with the giving of presents with much excitement and celebration. The staff were a witness to this. The girls seemed swept up in it. "You've got a Saints day haven't you, Miss?" said Miriam, backed up by some of the others. Taken aback I couldn't think what they meant. "Oh, you mean Saint David, the Patron Saint of Wales," I said. "It's not quite the same, we don't worship or pray to our Saint and he is the Saint for the whole of Wales, but he is still important to us as Welsh people." This seemed to satisfy them. I decided that at the first opportunity I would brush up on the history of Dewi Sant (Saint David), just in case. Just as well I did.

On the morning of March the first, waiting for the girls to come in to Assembly, I was surprised to see that a few of them were carrying a single daffodil which they presented to me in a solemn manner. "Happy Saint's Day, Miss," they chorused. I was very touched, but I didn't think that Jim the Head Gardener would feel the same way when he saw that his daffodil beds had been desecrated! There was more to come. "Now, perhaps we could hear the history of this special saint," called out Sister Mary from the other side of the room, as she came forward and settled down to hear my "talk." Just as well I was prepared, as I had expected something like this to happen as the nuns had a sneaky habit of catching us unawares. I received a burst of applause at the end. It all seemed a bit surreal.

I was all set to attend my first family meeting, held regularly on site. The outcome of such a meeting was that a decision would be made on the future of the child. The group consisted of the child, the parent(s) or guardians, their Social worker, key worker, and school tutor.

Today it was Stacey who sat demurely next to her key worker, whilst the Social worker began by reporting on the progress she felt Stacey had made. Tension was high and remained so as we all gave our reports. Mine was on her general progress in school, ending with a personal account of her attitude and behaviour. On the whole she enjoyed school and behaved accordingly. If she enjoyed a subject she worked with fury taking it all in. She was an intelligent child.

As Stacey gave her report, I watched her mother's face change as she guessed what her daughter was about to suggest. "I want to go home, perhaps for weekends or something," Stacey said. Her mother's reply was straight. "I can't have you home, my nerves are too bad, the doctor says so." Her face hardened and her daughter's crumpled. Stacey had been put into care as a child being out of control. She had been in trouble with the police for minor offences, run away on a couple of occasions and been generally disruptive at home. Mother was having no more of it which she made very plain, and as there was no Father figure in evidence the decision was solely hers. Stacey was fourteen and a half, and the outcome would be she would remain at Ravenscourt for the foreseeable future. She was led away in distress by her keyworker.

Sometimes after an amiable discussion a parent or

parents were encouraged to stay in the flat at the top of the building for a night, but not so on this occasion. I left feeling quite shaken, this was my first but would not be my last meeting of this kind, as unbeknown to me there was worse to come!

One morning Mary-Ann joined us. Much discussion had taken place between the Sisters and staff in preparation for this. None of us knew what to expect as we had been given no guidance on how to proceed, so we decided to play it by ear! We realised she would not know what to expect either, so it would be a learning curve for all of us.

She arrived surprisingly "dressed down" in jeans and a jumper. I thought it would have been more appropriate for her to have worn slightly more formal clothes, or perhaps she saw herself as fitting in with the students? The plan was for her to join classes in order to see what was going on. She fitted in quite well taking it all in her stride. I thought at the time it would have been better if she had joined the Care staff programme, as it eventually turned out she became involved in the ferrying to and fro of girls who were involved in the local sports programmes, always of course accompanied by a member of staff.

She eventually became an important member of the team at Ravenscourt. We discovered she was a warm and caring person and the girls took to her. "She's alright, that posh girl" they were heard to say. Most of them were from London's East End or other London boroughs; so

Mary-Ann's dulcet tones were somewhat alien to them, but later on it was "Mary-Ann said this," or "Mary-Ann said that."

During the time that the Sisters ran Ravenscourt, many invitations to shows and events in London were issued. One such treat was an invitation from London's Apollo Theatre with tickets to see Andrew Lloyd-Webber's Rock Musical Starlight Express. The trip was arranged and planned with great excitement. On the day ten girls and three teachers piled into the mini-bus. On the way we overheard "I hope this won't be boring?" and "It might be alright I suppose," and unexpectedly "I expect it will be okay."

As we settled down in the dress circle seats, a voice was heard to say "Free hats for all at Ravenscourt School."

'Oh no,' I thought rather ungratefully, 'not again, drawing attention to us.' I need not have worried as the girls took it well and held their hands out for what was offered, which was a black baseball cap emboldened with silver "Starlight Express" on the front. "Nice," "These are good," "Nice of them," was heard, but strangely enough, after we had all tried them on for size, they were put away in bags, never to be seen again! I later wore mine for gardening! A good time was had by all.

The comments on the return journey were positive as the girls muttered in turn, "That was okay." "The hats are nice," "I'll give mine to my little brother," and "I wouldn't mind going again to these show things."

For the most part, it was a pleasure taking the girls

out, as their behaviour was usually quite good, and of course the free tickets were much appreciated.

CHAPTER FOUR

Dawn, aged 16 was one of the older girls and as such, felt some responsibility towards the younger ones. She was 16 going on 21 and she looked older than her age. She worked diligently in class and was always polite and well-mannered. It was always "Thanks, Miss," or "Okay, Miss," so it was quite a shock when we discovered one morning that she had run away.

I had still to learn that this behaviour was part of a pattern to be expected by children who found themselves in care through no fault of their own. Many of them had consistently run away from home, trying to escape from a neglectful environment. The Care Staff, after contacting the Social worker had pursued every avenue to try and find her, but with no luck. The police were finally called and we felt there was nothing further to do but wait.

After many weeks it was announced that the Police

had found Dawn. We were horrified to learn that she had been found in a London hotel prostituting herself to wealthy businessmen from overseas. She was 16, so obviously thought it was alright. How it all came to happen did not bear thinking about. She said very little on the matter, only that her cousin had taken her up to London. We were told that "of course she would not be returning to Ravenscourt, but that she would be sent to a lock-up. She was eventually sent to a Secure Unit in an Outer London Borough.

Lindy was coming up to her 15th birthday, and she had been talking about it for weeks. "I'm nearly 15, not far from 16 now." She was a delightful girl of African origin and small in stature who talked incessantly, sometimes with exaggeration, sometimes stories with no foundation. Her House Mother was organising a party for her to celebrate, and I was very surprised and touched to receive an invitation. I pondered, 'what would I give her as a gift?' and decided on flowers. Still wondering if it would be appropriate, I turned up on the birthday evening with Chrysanthemums. As it happened, I needn't have worried. Lindy came forward to greet her guests and her face lit up as she saw what I was carrying. "I haven't ever got flowers before, Miss" she chortled. I remember my feelings of pleasure and warmth at her response to my gift.

We were surprised one morning when Sister Angela sailed into the Staff room and announced without any preamble "I have arranged for my teachers to attend a

Stress Course, next Tuesday, so there will be no classes on that day." She gave no further information as she probably didn't know anything more about it, then she sailed out. I am all for the continuation of staff training but was rather surprised at the training chosen. We just stared at each other. "Does she think that we look all that stressed?" I said.

Nothing more was said as we got on with the day's work. And as there was only a few days to go until the day of the course we did not have a lot of time to discuss it. As time went on we became quite cross that we were given no preparation notes or ideas on what to expect. The Care staff were taking the girls out for the day, having told them that the day was a Teachers Study Day. Somehow they got wind of what was going on. Questions were asked. "What are you having a stress day for? "Are we making you all stressed?" "Were you stressed before?" When they challenged me I was not prepared to discuss the matter and replied "The answer to all those questions is NO of course not, carry on with your work." They had to be satisfied with that.

By the time we arrived in the staff room on Tuesday, we found the chairs arranged in a semi-circle. The tutor's notes, books and a white board stood at the ready. Dr Cane was a friendly individual, and after his introduction to us by Sister Angela he proceeded. We were soon put at ease by his body language, or so I thought. "What is stress?" he began. No answer from us "Are any of you stressed?" was the next question. "No," we chorused. As we felt this was true. "Then why are you all sitting with your arms tightly folded across your chests?" Looking around we watched each other quickly move our arms to a more relaxed position. "Stress is the non- specific response of the body to any demand made upon it." He informed us.

The day was hard work as we jointly and singly explored our reactions, feelings, attitudes and expectations, but was nevertheless enjoyable. What did we get out of it? We certainly learnt more about each other, ourselves and the possible feelings and emotions of the girls. Whether or not this made us better teachers, who knows?

The girls were for the most part intelligent, and in spite of their horrendous backgrounds, they saw learning as important to their future lives. It also came out quite casually from time to time that they seemed to be amazingly forgetful of any horrors and wanted their Mum, Dad, Gran to be proud of them.

They worked well at any given task and we wanted to give them something to aim for. We had all been used to 'O and A level exams which had been introduced in 1951 replacing the 16+ School Certificate. CSE'S were introduced in 1965. There was some excitement about the new GCSE's that were introduced in 1986 in replacement. It was felt that our girls would stand a better chance of success with the continuous course work instead of sitting exams. Along with RSA exams in Commercial work this did prove to work very well.

All was going quite well at Ravenscourt. We had

formed good relationships with members of the Care staff especially as informal discussions were had on a regular basis. As teaching staff we were interested in how things were going in the girls' home environment, and they were keen to hear how things were progressing at school. One or two of the girls were allowed home at the weekend, depending on the home circumstances. Others went to short term Foster Carers who had been carefully chosen, approved and trained. Others stayed at the units, where the staff tried to make the time pleasurable for them by arranging outings.

There were quarrels amongst the girls just as there was amongst siblings in families. Sometimes the arguments were petty, others were more serious and took on a personal note, sorted out satisfactorily without any outside involvement such as the Social Worker.

One Tuesday morning we were in the Teacher's staff room, looking forward to the week ahead when the door burst open and a voice called out. "Emergency community meeting in ten minutes." We simultaneously raised eyebrows and questions arose immediately. 'Why was Jannette the school secretary calling us? Why was Sister Angela absent from giving us the usual 'pep talk'? There had been several community meetings before to discuss matters concerning minor misdemeanours, but these had always been planned in advance. This must indeed be serious.

We filed into the hall where care staff and girls were already seated in the usual large circle. I wondered, not for the first time, why we were seated in this way. One always expected something to happen in the circle, Sister Mary doing a dance, wimple flying perhaps? It never did. I chided myself.

I tried to guess by the body language of all those seated, to see what could possibly be the problem, I was soon to know. As Head of Ravenscourt, Sister Mary began. "I have called this meeting as I am very upset that Sister Angela my Head of Education, has been assaulted by one of our pupils here at Ravenscourt." It was easy to see by now that the culprit was a tiny redhead called Gemma who was shrinking in her chair, where she appeared even smaller. At last the victim spoke up "I was visiting the unit last evening when I encountered Gemma in the kitchen, where she threw a large pot of ice-cream over me."

Was that it I thought? The vision in my mind of little Gemma with her open pot of ice-cream, for that's what it was attacking large bulky Sister Angela made me want to giggle. Sister Angela went on, and on, repeating much of the same. She wasn't hurt in the least. Her pride was damaged, or maybe it was the mucking up of her wimple that bothered her? I lost interest as we had much more important things to be getting on with. However, I brought myself back to the problem in hand. "What do you have to say for yourself Gemma?" asked Sister Mary. The Sisters never shouted, but always seemed to remain calm. What they didn't say at any one time was ominous!

"Nothing" replied Gemma." I wondered was there anyone who could provide evidence in support of her. The child must have been provoked as she was a quiet girl and I had never seen any obvious bad behaviour from her.

Was that it, can we get into class now? , I pondered. No such luck. "I want all members of staff here to make a comment on this kind of behaviour" Said Sister Mary. Looking across at the sheer numbers in the room, it looked as though this might take until break time at least. Gemma's behaviour was totally unacceptable and she should receive some sort of punishment, but surely this could have been handled at a personal level and not involved the rest of us?

Members of staff raised a hand at random to show they were ready to speak. To my horror most of them did not have a good word to say about Gemma, although a number of them did not say anything and I decided I would be one of them. It seemed to me that some of the staff were keen to keep in with the Sisters as many of the comments were inane pointless ones, such as "she is often cheeky when asked to do chores" Well what teenager isn't?

Finally it was decided that her punishment would be delayed and we were allowed to have a break, followed by lessons as usual. That's that then I thought, the end of any involvement by the teachers. When classes resumed I expected to hear the girls chattering amongst themselves about this 'serious matter' but nothing was said. I found this very strange.

Personally, I had not heard the end of it. I was called into Sister Angela's study later that day. She got straight to the point. "I am very disappointed in you. You were the only one of my teachers who did not support me." She repeated it as if I hadn't heard "You didn't say a word." I was dumfounded. I had always got on well with Sister Angela.

I replied "To be honest I thought that the girl had been through enough with all the negative comments that had already been made. I decided not to add to it. That's all I can say. I'm sorry if you feel that way." She accepted my reason and replied "Well, we'll say no more about it" She did not appear to feel any ill will towards me from then on, so it was a best forgotten confrontation as far as I was concerned.

I had shared my faith with a few of the girls who were interested as they knew I attended church on Sunday. From time to time they would ask me to "pray for me, Miss," with a bit of a smirk. Imagine my surprise when one day three of them came to me and asked "Can we come to church with you sometime, Miss?" "Of course as I am Jewish I don't believe in that Jesus stuff, but it's the same God I think," announced Miriam, who was very proud of her heritage.

Arrangements were made with Care staff in that Shirley would bring them over to my house, stay for tea and return to the unit. The rest of us would attend the evening service at our local Baptist Church, then my husband and I would take them back home after the service.

The Sunday arrived and Shirley and the girls arrived in time for tea. During tea I mentioned that Cliff Richard visited our church on a regular basis and might be there this evening. "Oh," said Sarah, "me Mum is a big fan of his; she seen him once on stage, can we get a picture of him for me mum?" Michelle was not bothered, and Miriam said nothing. I warned the girls that if they did see Cliff they were not to say anything to him; we treated him just like any other member of the congregation at church.

The girls seemed to enjoy the service as they kept very quiet, listening to everything that was going on, and enjoying the singing. I think they were overawed by the sheer size of the congregation, which was over 300 people of all ages.

When the service was over, we went into the side hall for coffee where I introduced the girls to other members of the congregation as "My Students" before giving their names. This seemed to please them.

"Isn't Cliff here?" asked Sarah. There had been no sign of him, but as the congregation numbered over 300 at any evening service it was not surprising as Cliff always kept a low profile. We were in the vestibule preparing to go home when who should stride along minding his own business was Cliff. Sarah approached him.

"Hello Cliff," she said in a loud voice. I held my breath.

"Hello," he replied with a smile and carried on walking. All three girls now decided they would like a signed photo, so I promised I would see what I could do. One of the members of Cliff's backing group at that time was a Church member along with his wife and two small children. As I knew the wife quite well and was teaching the children in Sunday School at the time, I didn't think it would be too much of a problem to obtain a signed photograph of the Star. I mentioned it the following Sunday, and within two weeks I gave the three girls a signed personal copy of Cliff. They were delighted.

School carried on without too many problems. What problems I encountered were minor and could be dealt with on the spot. The girls worked well and supported each other to a certain extent, although there was no friendship grouping, with each girl appearing to want to keep her independence. I sensed a fear in them of allowing too close a friendship.

I realised more and more as the days went by that I really enjoyed this job as did the other teachers. We had formed a strong group and were very supportive of each other. Also a bond of friendship had developed. We met one another out of school hours for meals and visits to the theatre.

CHAPTER FIVE

One day Lindy announced that plans were in hand for a visit to attend a concert given by the London Community Gospel Choir. Looking straight at me she said "you can come too Miss if you like, and your 'usband." The Care staff were organising the outing and already tickets had been bought.

The Choir had been formed in 1982 by the Reverend Basil Meade and was receiving rave reviews. Lindy interrupted my thoughts. "My cousin is in the choir so that's why I am looking forward to it so much." Oh yes, I thought, here goes Lindy on one of her fantasies.

The evening arrived. We all sat together in the stalls. The concert took place at the Empire Pool Wembley and was a wonderful evening, the singing, the body language of the singers, and the glittering attire of the singers was simply captivating. The women wore black dresses covered with coloured sequins which shimmered in the lights, with the men dressed also in black, their ties matching the women's dresses.

Unfortunately, the end came too soon, the lights came up and we prepared to leave. Imagine my surprise when Lindy came over and said to me "My cousin has invited me backstage. We can't all go but you can come if you like, Miss." We did and it was delightful. The choir were so friendly and happy and made a big fuss of Lindy. I felt ashamed that I had doubted Lindy when she had been so proud in telling me of her relationship to one of the singers.

The blow came one day, when Elli one of the younger teachers announced "I'm pregnant, so I'm afraid I will be leaving you in due course." She was obviously thrilled about it so the rest of us congratulated her, as we tried to hide our dismay. Thoughts ran through my head; will she be returning? Will we get a temp? Elli taught Home Economics, and there were plenty of teachers around so I looked on the bright side.

I had spent some time thinking of Dawn who was now in a Secure Unit on the other side of London. After discussion with the Care staff who had been working with her, I decided I would visit her in the Secure Unit. The Social worker was contacted and promised to ask her if she would like a visit from me, she said yes, so a visit was planned for the following week.

I arrived with some trepidation despite the building looking unthreatening with its white walls and green painted door. I was greeted with the usual pleasantries by a friendly woman who invited me in. "My name is Catherine" she announced. "I am in charge of the wing that Dawn is in." One or two people were walking about. I couldn't tell their age as their heads were bent down as if in desperation. Or perhaps it was my imagination?

Taking the lift to the third floor we arrived at another green painted door. Upon knocking, the door was opened by another woman, older and stockier this time, and looking like a person not to be trifled with, but her attitude towards me was a friendly one, as she smiled and welcomed me inside saying "Hello, my name is Marie." I was then shocked to see that at the end of the room there was a locked iron gate which she unlocked into another corridor which led eventually to the room that Dawn was in.

Dawn was sitting in a corner chair, but got up as I entered. "I'll leave you two to chat, but first would you like a cup of tea?" asked Marie. I accepted gratefully. At last I was able to sit down next to Dawn. "How are you?" was all I could manage.

"Or right I s'pose" she replied. My heart went out to her locked in this room. It was comfortable with a TV, books etc. but she looked so forlorn. On the surface it appeared that it was entirely her own fault for seeking out bad company and getting into the state she was found in, but I found myself sympathising with her as in desperation she had succumbed to the charms of her much older so called cousin who had led her astray in the first place. These children are so desperate for love and attention, having received very little in their young lives.

She asked "How's school?" And on that common ground we managed to have a chat. "Me, Mum an' sister have been," she said. "I'm only here for a bit till they know what to do with me."

I had taken her a small gift of scented soap, and she was very pleased. Suddenly it was time for me to leave and I wondered whether my visit had done any good, but she did say "Thanks for coming, Miss" and took hold of my hand. I was touched at this. I knew I would not see her again as she would not be returning to Ravenscourt, but I wished her all the best for the future, and prayed that a lovely girl like her, with her intelligence had a chance of a good future if she looked for it.

Sister Angela called me into her room one day. 'Oh, I wonder what's up?' I thought. She greeted me with a smile as she said "I have a proposition for you. I was wondering, as I like the school to be forward looking, whether we should get computers?"

I was excited and even though it would be a lot of work for me, as I would have to learn the workings of one first of all, I agreed at once. Sister Angela had already done some background work, she had the details over which we had a long discussion, particularly around the Amstrad Word Processor and printer had been launched in September 1985. I was sent off to the local Electrical shop, where a demonstration had been arranged for me. I found it very interesting and informative. I looked forward to learning this new skill and passing on my knowledge to the girls.

I reported back and four Word Processors were ordered and delivered. I took one home to familiarize myself with the workings and found I was delighted with this new skill. The girls were very impressed when they saw the machines on the desks. I had typed out a Learners Guide for each student and was amazed at how quickly they took to it. Some of them were already proficient in typewriting and had passed an RSA Elementary examination. I had high hopes of a Word Processing examination for some of these girls. "Easy peasy, Miss" said one bright spark, and the others in the group, not wanting to feel less clever, agreed wholeheartedly. The ones who decided to learn the skill, did very well, several of them passing examinations in due course.

As the weather improved we began planning a Summer Sports Day. The two units, joined by all members of staff and the Sisters started practising. The girls loved it.

The sports day dawned, warm and sunny. There was such a crowd. All members of staff, care workers, teachers, office staff and gardeners, even those off duty, including the cooks were prepared to join in.

There was Janet, complete with whistle, leading the sports, and the rest of us doing our bit. But where were the girls from the unit in the grounds? Suddenly there came a loud singing "here we go, here we go, here we go," and from behind the massive oak tree the girls appeared, led by a member of Care staff. Robin was a young man, a new recruit and very popular with both staff and girls. Also a member of the local Rugby team, he had borrowed all their shirts and shorts for the girls to wear. This resulted in lots of cheering and clapping and got the day started on a splendid note, followed by an egg and spoon race, sack race, throw the welly and a relay race. All went very well with Janet handing out the replica cups she had bought to the worthy winners. The cooks had surpassed themselves providing jugs of fresh lemonade, sandwiches and cakes. All agreed it had been a great day, and one that should be repeated each year from now on.

As the previous day trip to London had been so successful, the teachers had planned a further day out, taking a picnic and travelling by train to West Kensington station, followed by the short walk up Exhibition Road to Hyde Park and the Lido. Nine girls and four staff set off on a lovely day. The train journey was uneventful and we arrived at our destination in good time for lunch, after which we all had ice-creams which were very welcome as the sun was beating down. Just the weather for a nice cool swim, so we made our way to the Lido which was very busy with swimmers and sunbathers.

We had broached the subject of swimming costumes with the girls before we left. "I ain't takin me gear off for nobody," stated Jenny firmly. "We ain't neither, no way" the others echoed. As we adults were not swimming either, we decided to watch, as there was a lot going on. Then looking casually to the left I noticed several people sunbathing in the nude! They were right in the corner so could not cause offence or be particularly noticed or so I thought. Janet and I looked at each other and nodding in agreement we led our little group in the opposite direction. We were too late! "One of the girls yelled at the top of her voice, "Hey, Miss, there's people over there with no clothes on," followed by one or two of the others making comments also.

"They mus' be freezing."

"Why are they doing that?"

It was obvious that the girls weren't laughing or making fun as some of them looked really perturbed at the scene. It suddenly struck me that due to their horrendous backgrounds, maybe they associated the scene with sex. We tried to explain that there are groups of people who sunbathe in this way, and that it was quite natural for them, but the girls didn't seem convinced. Eventually they got bored with the matter, and another ice-cream was mentioned and that was that.

We eventually made our way back to the train station, as we wanted to get away before peak travelling time. Walking along the passage leading to the trains we heard music. The usual buskers. One young man was playing the guitar really well and we stood for a few seconds to listen. To my surprise the girls started rummaging in bags, with each one bringing out a few coppers which they placed in his cap. "Thanks," they said, quietly for them. "An the music's not bad either."

I didn't say anything, but I was full of admiration for them as they put us adults to shame. We arrived back at our local station to be met by the minibus. The girls started relating stories of the day. "You know Jim, we saw lots of people with no clothes on in London." A statement that certainly needed some explanation!

Time was going on for the appointment of a new teacher of Home Economics. The Sisters had been busy advertising the post and sifting through the application forms. He or she would have to be appointed in good time for the start of the new term in September. Eventually a short list of four had been decided, and the applicants called for interview. The Sisters discussed the applicants with us teachers. Imagine my surprise when one of them was a teacher of my acquaintance from my days working in an Adult Education Institute. I immediately thought, 'Oh, no,' as what I knew of her she was an excellent teacher, very personable, well qualified, and was running a Home Economics Department already. Her teaching method however, was very rigid, with little or no flexibility, as in her insistence on a student cleaning the cooker thoroughly before moving on to the next task had been well-known throughout the Institute. Unfortunately, as I couldn't see her fitting in with our girls. I informed the Sisters of my concerns.

The interviews took place and the person chosen "as she was the best qualified and experienced" was Anne, the teacher of my acquaintance. 'So much for my advice' I thought. 'Perhaps it will work out, I certainly hope so.'

As it was nearly lunchtime and I was tidying away the books I was surprised that Sandra one of the girls was hovering about. What was she up to? I wondered as they usually couldn't wait to get away for their lunch. "Can I help you, Sandra?" I asked.

After some hesitation she blurted out "You're going to hate me, Miss, when I tell you."

"Out with it then" I said. "It can't be that bad!"

"I'm pregnant and I'm goin' to have an abortion." I was taken aback that she should have told me at all as she was not a girl who was especially friendly with me. She seemed to mistake my silence for disapproval. "What with you bein' religious an all," she continued. I hastened to reassure her.

"Of course I don't hate you Sandra. If that is what you and your Social worker have decided is the best thing for you to do, that's OK by me." Sandra was almost 17 and spent occasional week-ends with Foster Carers. She left the room quietly but looked satisfied with my reply. My heart went out to her. She did have the abortion a week later, having a week off school, and returning as though she had been on holiday. I felt relieved that she seemed well adjusted and worked well in class as usual.

The girls enjoyed the Religious Education lessons which I taught once a week, which included Comparative Religion where we enjoyed visits by a Buddhist, a Muslim, and representatives of other faiths. Of course the Roman Catholic faith was prominent amongst us as there were five of the Sisters who wore the habit and who worked amongst us. On one occasion the girls were critical of faith in general saying "What good do these guys do, all this believing thing an' that." I was caught off guard. I began to tell them about the work that was being done both at home and overseas in the name of Religious communities both Christian and non-Christian. "UNICEF (United Nations Children's Fund) is the largest," I said.

"Can you bring something to show us about them?" asked Sarah with the others showing interest also. I was very touched when they unanimously said "We want to help too."

The next day I brought in leaflets showing the work of UNICEF. To my great pleasure and surprise they had brought money. "Can you send this for the children?" We there and then composed a letter to UNICEF UK.

"Who is going to type this then?" I queried. As I knew she would, before any of the others had a chance Sarah volunteered. "I'm the best typist, I will." So she did and the letter was sent off with a cheque for the money. A week later we received a lovely letter from UNICEF thanking the girls for their generosity and enclosing a leaflet showing pictures of the children they had helped all around the world. There were smiles all round. The letter was pinned up on the Hall noticeboard, so that it could be read by all who entered the building. In the midst of their own problems, these girls once again had amazed me by thinking of the problems of others.

Elli had left to have her baby and Anne had now

begun teaching Home Economics in her place. We realised how difficult it would be for her to fit into an established group, especially one such as ours, and we did all we could to make her feel welcome especially on her first day. "I know you, don't I?" she queried, looking at me quite relieved to see a friendly face. "I didn't know you worked here. What's it like?" Everyone joined in and explained the many advantages of working in a Care setup, the job satisfaction, but also the difficulties we sometimes experience. She seemed relieved that we all seemed a happy bunch of teachers.

CHAPTER SIX

The call came at 7.30am on a Monday morning. 'Who on earth can this be this time in the morning' I said to myself.

A rather strained voice said "This is Jannette."

What could the School Secretary possibly want at this time in the morning?

"If you aren't sitting down sit down now," she insisted. "I have some terrible news to tell you, Catherine is dead. She inhaled hairspray. I am making sure that all staff know before they turn up at school."

I didn't know what to think. Was this some cruel joke? Of course not, I chided myself. I shared the news with my husband as he was setting off for work.

I arrived at school early. A number of staff were already assembled in the Main Hall. The Principal Sister Mary, Sister Angela, and Sister Winnifred one of the other Sisters, plus many Care staff. The girls came in later one or two at a time accompanied by their Key workers. We were all in a state of shock. Catherine was an Irish girl, quiet, hardworking and compared with some of the others, no trouble at all.

A number of the girls spent week-ends away with family members or at placements so Care staff numbers were minimum. Through her tears and supported by the Sisters, Nia, Catherine's Care Worker explained what had happened "Sunday afternoon, Catherine decided she would take a bath. I helped her get her stuff together. She liked her bath, and as she didn't have any of her friends around that day, I knew she would take a while. She put her radio on, and I left the room, telling her not to lock the door. I kept going back and forth to the bathroom door. The radio was still playing loudly, but as the girls value their privacy, I didn't call out. After about 25 minutes, I thought the water must be getting cold, so I called out "are you alright?" I got no reply. I called again louder this time, still no reply. I started banging on the door and by now I was frightened, and the door was locked. In a panic I ran downstairs to call Jim the gardener, who was working overtime in the gardening workshop. With brute force he managed to wrench open the door where we found Catherine slumped in the bath. There was no sign of life and we feared the worst."

The rest of the day, in fact the next few days, passed in a daze as we tried to carry on with our regular routines, all the while trying to provide some comfort to the girls.

We were not really aware of all the comings and goings behind the scenes as we waited for the result of the post-mortem. Catherine had sprayed a dangerous amount of hairspray at the back of her throat and this had caused a cardiac arrest. The verdict was 'Death by misadventure.'

The Sisters were planning the funeral, and as Catherine's quite extensive family were Roman Catholic, the funeral would take place in the Roman Catholic Church. We had all tried to keep some sort of normality during the time building up to the funeral. I was impressed by the attitude of the girls as they tried to comfort each other and the adults trying to help them.

The day of the funeral arrived and we all trouped down to the church which was a short walk away. We were a sombre group. Many people had come to pay their respects. All the Ravenscourt staff of course, in some cases accompanied by members of their own families, some of whom had known Catherine. Also many folk of the town had turned up. We settled in our seats, hankies at the ready. We were sure to need them. We had been told that many relatives and friends were coming over from Ireland to attend the funeral. There seemed to be dozens of them. They filled up three rows each side of the aisle, all dressed in black and sniffing loudly. In spite of myself I felt angry. Where were any of them in Catherine's hour of need? The coffin entered and we were broken.

The service was very well conducted by the Priest, and the flowers were lovely, but I sat through it in a daze as I'm sure did many others. We returned to Ravenscourt where refreshments were laid out for the visitors. The teachers returned to school, preparing ourselves in counselling mode should the girls prefer to return to lessons, which some of them did.

School continued, the hard workers continued as before, the others to work at their own pace. At our weekly meetings we discussed ways of taking the girls out for further Educational trips, or putting on interesting events to cheer them up during the months leading up to winter.

CHAPTER SEVEN

An invitation came for a number of us to attend a Photographic studio in London where a firm was launching a disposable camera, one of the first of its kind. We didn't know what to expect. We piled into the mini-bus which took us to a bustling studio in London's West End. There were a number of people in charge of the event, rushing around carrying cameras, tripods and other gear.

We were each given a tiny disposable camera and taught how to use it. Other people were milling around. It all seemed a bit disorganized, so we just did as we were told, kept snapping. It was all good fun; quite noisy with everyone talking quite loudly.

A voice called extra loudly, "I know you don't I, I seen you on the telly, something crittins ain't it?"

It was Bernard Cribbins, who was high profile in the 80s. "And you are?" he replied with a smile.

"I'm Michelle" she said rather shyly, now the attention was fully on her. He obviously knew who our group was, and joined in the fun we were having, allowing us to take pictures of him. Lunch was provided, and an enjoyable day was had by all.

I had spent some time planning a Fancy Dress party, thinking it would cheer us all up during the winter months. With the cooperation of the care staff it was held in one of the units. The assortment of gear and the painting of faces were quite impressive. One bag lady complete with headscarf, grubby cardigan and plastic bags. Several "I don't know who I'm meant to be but I look fantastic." They were wearing an assortment of long dresses, with heavy makeup and wigs. Trying to look like film stars maybe? There were two clowns, and three tarts. The girls had all got together to swap ideas.

Sian had whispered to me a few days before the event. "I'm not coming, I got nothing to wear." Never 'one of the gang' I could understand where she was coming from. However I had an idea. "How about if I bring in my Welsh costume, would you like to wear that?" I expected her to pull a face, but her face lit up. "Yes, I'd like that," was her reply. The Welsh hat was a little too small, the shawl too tight, as was the apron around her plump waist, but she was happy. "I think I look Welsh," she commented with delight.

We played games, and the food was good. There was no prize for the best fancy dress; I told them they all looked fantastic and gave them a chocolate bar each. They were quite pleased, and so was I that the evening had been a success.

During the renovation of the building, the Sisters had taken over a small corner on the ground floor, away from the classrooms, and fashioned it into a Chapel. They worshipped at the local Roman Catholic Church, where they attended early morning Mass before most people got up in the mornings. The chapel within Ravenscourt was very private and was used by the sisters for prayer and spiritual meetings during the day. We did get a peep into this room in the early days and were quite impressed by what we saw. Little did I know that this special room would one day be my classroom. Deep mullion windows framed the room. There was a bright red carpet, plus centrally situated was a small Altar (Holy Table) on which the Priest celebrated the Holy Mass. Complete with two rows of chairs it looked quite splendid. There was the usual Crucifix on the wall and several icons depicting various Saints. A heavy brass key was always in the door during the day, only removed when it was locked at night.

I was just getting ready to dismiss the girls after an R.E. lesson when Sister Mary entered. "The Priest is coming tomorrow morning at 11.00a.m, to take Mass," she said. I wondered why on earth we would want to know this? She continued "I thought that you would all like to attend?" Looking around at the small group.

I said yes immediately, as this came over more like a command, and one did not disobey Sister. To my surprise the girls all looked pleased. I had noticed that since the funeral, the girls had shown an interest and a curiosity about the Catholic Church. Possibly this fact had filtered down to the Sisters, hence the invitation.

The following morning we all arrived. Michelle whispered to me "I got my best top on, Miss." The priest was already there in his robes looking splendid in a green and gold cassock. The four sisters were already seated, but Sister Mary came forward to show us to our seats. The service consisted of opening prayers, the reading of a psalm, a short talk by the Priest, and then preparation of the bread and wine for the Mass began. All the sisters lined up, and to my surprise so did the girls, saying as they did so "we are Catholics." As the priest approached them they each opened their mouths wide to receive "The Host" as if they had been doing it all their lives. The Sisters smiled in approval. It was an enjoyable service, and I felt honoured that we had been invited in to the Sisters "Special Place."

Dana had invited me to the unit for a cup of tea after school one day. It seemed so long ago since she had put her feet up on the desk and refused to work for me. We had now become friends, and I guessed she wanted to chat to me about her future.

The time was approaching when she would be leaving and plans were being put in place. As I settled into a comfy chair and sipped my tea, she confided her hopes. "I don't care what job I do so long as it's a good one; and well-paid of course." She had told me previously that due to her home situation being so bad at the time she had put all her belongings in a black plastic bag and put herself in Care. There was more to it than that of course, the Social Service wheels had been put in place but the fact was that she had to all intents and purposes put herself in Care. One of her sayings was "Me Nan's house is like Steptoe's back yard." For some reason she kept saying it as if there was a deep seated reason for such a statement. The comedy 'Steptoe and Son' was on the TV at the time. As she was now 17 there was a good chance she would be able to return to her home area, and she was hoping that she would be allocated social housing in the form of a small flat. Dana was from Romford, Essex and was keen to return to the area. Her relationship with her father appeared to be a good one and also she had friends there. She was already planning in her mind for this to happen even though nothing definite had been decided.

I was very surprised when she asked in an offhand manner "Can I keep in touch with you Miss when I've left?" I can let you know what I'm doing if you like." I felt quite touched at this request and replied that I would be very pleased to hear from her. As I was not prepared to give out my personal phone number at this stage I said "You can get hold of me through your Social Worker." She was quite happy with this.

One morning after lessons three of the girls hovered around my desk. Puzzled at this and wanting to go for my lunch I said "Off you go or your dinner will get cold."

"We want to tell you something, Miss," said Michelle. I replied "Out with it then."

"We been playing Wee-Gee board, what about that?" piped up Tara. After a bit more discussion with them, I realised that they meant an 'Ouija Board'. Never mind about lunch, this was serious stuff.

One of the biggest challenges facing the Christian Church today is the fact that thousands of people are interested in the supernatural, but rarely if ever associate it with the Ministry of the Church. Humankind still longs for something beyond the materialistic things of life, so they are seeking answers in the world of astrology, fortune telling, Spiritism, witchcraft and Satanism. There were a number of do-it-yourself kits available and this included the Ouija Board. Many people see this 'game' as a bit of fun.

In the short time available I explained the possible dangers and pitfalls of being involved in such activities.

"We thought we might hear from Catherine, and she might tell us how she is getting on," said Tina.

I realised then what might have set them off on this path. I was concerned also that they refused to tell me who the person was that had given this 'game' as they had obviously seen it. I made an appointment with them to have a further talk on the matter the following day. I spread the word about this and invited anyone who was interested to join us on the following day at the allotted time.

I was pleasantly surprised that on the following day the three girls turned up as planned, as I had half expected them to continue seeing the whole episode as a bit of fun. Accompanying them was four more, each one of these girls presenting a contrived look of boredom as so often happened when an arrangement was not of their own making. This particular look was them saying "look, I don't have to be here, but I've come so I'd better make the best of it." I was by now quite used to this act so did not feel at all perturbed by it. They settled down and I began by showing them a magazine I had brought along which meant nothing to them, it was only a book after all. They had been already told many lies in their short lives it would be difficult to convince them of the dangers of the kind of activity they had been involved in so I thought I would do my best by relating a true story I had brought along.

During the 80s the famous Disc Jockey Kenny Everett was warning people of the dangers of playing with an Ouija board, which was commonly known as The Spirit of the Glass.

Originally printed as a magazine article, and later printed in book form TALK OF THE DEVIL. Everett related the true story of two of his friends who visited his home one night. After supper they decided to have 'some fun' and try out an experiment with the board.

They set up the board in the usual way. They placed the glass which was turned upside down in the middle of the board which has the letters of the alphabet arranged in a semi-circle with the words 'yes' and 'no' at either end. They each placed a finger on the glass and proceeded to ask the 'spirit' questions. His friend Raymond was told that a girl had a message for him and the name 'JANEY' was spelt out. "That can't be true," said Raymond. "The only Janey I know is a close friend. I saw her yesterday, and she was alive and well, so the message can't be from her." We asked the 'spirit' when she had died and were shocked when the glass spelled out 'noon today.' Raymond then gasped out "where are you now?" The glass spelled out 'Mortuary 'and gave the address of one a few miles away.

By now they were all badly shaken and Raymond was persuaded to telephone the mortuary, who told him the details the glass had told them were true. All four of them were in a terrible state by now, especially as the last words the glass had spelled out, supposedly from Janey were 'JOIN ME'. With trembling hands all four carried the board outside and chopped it up into many pieces. The Disc Jockey had many outlets to the general public through his work on Radio and resolved that he would tell as many people as possible of the terrible dangers of dabbling in things they didn't understand and couldn't control.

By now the girls were looking frightened at what they had heard. "Any questions?" I asked. There was no reply.

I didn't really expect them to react. I don't know what I expected really! As time was up I dismissed them and told them I was always available to discuss the matter further with them. The girls whispered together on the way out, and one of them called out "We won't be doing Wee-gee board any more, Miss." I was relieved to hear this but wasn't sure whether or not to believe them. I realised that I was quite shaken myself after relating this story.

CHAPTER EIGHT

The new Home Economics teacher was coping well as far as the rest of the teaching staff could see. If she had any problems she did not share them; during break time she usually stayed in her classroom. At lunchtime she usually went home as she only lived a short drive away. We tried to encourage her to join us but with no success. We decided that maybe complete independence was her preferred way of teaching, this being more in tune with teaching in an Adult Education Institute than in a CHE (Community Home with Education). It was just completely alien to us as we considered sharing of problems and difficulties to be part of the growing process in this type of work, and also beneficial to the girls we were teaching.

In complete contrast to students of the same ages in main stream education, the Ravenscourt girls did not play one teacher off against the other, they very rarely mentioned the name of one teacher to another. I found this very refreshing, as I did not have to justify my own or another teacher's behaviour or actions.

It was therefore not a complete surprise when we were informed by Sister Mary that Anne had given in her notice, and would be leaving at the end of term. She said no more, obviously she did not want any discussion on the 'why's' as she disappeared through the door. However, the rest of the teachers did want to discuss it. Feelings of guilt were uppermost to begin with. "Where had we gone wrong, what could we have done to improve matters for her?" I could never verbalise it at the time of course, but later I did say smugly to myself "I did say at the time of interview, that because of her previous background in teaching only in Adult Education, I did not think she would fit in. (Not very kind of me!) Once again there was a problem for the management who would have to re-advertise the post and elect another candidate.

A day out at the seaside was planned for ten of the girls and five members of staff. On this occasion it was two teachers and two care staff plus Sister Angela. Luckily it was not the job of the teachers to choose the girls who were to go on trips. That was the job of the care staff who always managed to successfully work out the numbers, as sometimes there were girls who did not want to go, but they were usually kept happy by a promise that there were other occasions when they could attend.

I counted myself one of the lucky ones on this

occasion. Having been brought up in a seaside town in South Wales, I loved the sea. The mini-bus was ordered for the day. We were ordered to bring a packed lunch and a swimsuit. Sister Angela was giving the orders. As Head of Education, she was a good sport, and joined in all the activities.

The big day arrived and we all piled into the minibus. The journey was uneventful and we arrived at the sandy beach with high expectations. The weather was warm and sunny and we settled ourselves on rugs.

There were exclamations of "Oh, it's dangerous," "Will it come up and drown us?" and other comments, mainly referring to the sea.

I hadn't realised that many of the girls had never seen the seaside before having come from Inner London areas. Their whole young lives so far had been centred in London and the inner and outer regions of the capital.

After much persuasion the girls put on swimsuits but all insisted on keeping on their t-shirts. Tara who was one of the older girls and always ready to confront staff, always very courteously, went bravely up to Sister Angela "Where's your cossi, Sister?" she asked and was rewarded with a smile. She was probably encouraged in her bravery by the fact that Sister Angela was wearing "civvies", which consisted of the leaving off of the wimple and donning a navy cover-up dress with a white collar. Sister Angela did this from time to time when attending casual events with the girls and staff, and as she was quite young I'm sure this action was approved by her superior Sister Mary. Also I privately thought that the leaving off of the wimple enabled the rest of us to see her mid-length lovely raven-black hair which she was obviously proud of, and this was very endearing.

We had organized races along the beach and much paddling had taken place, although the girls had a fear of venturing very far into the sea. The sheer size of the ocean frightened them as they were only used to the confined space of the local swimming baths. They shared their packed lunches and were showing a relaxed side of their nature by their communication with each other and the staff. After the moans when they couldn't remove the sand from their shoes, they all agreed that the new beach experience was "Good," "Okay," and "Quite okay," which was in line with their never show excitement or be overenthusiastic over anything attitude.

These occasions always brought the best out in the girls. Away from the home/school environment, relationships and communication skills were improved, confidence was built, and it was a learning curve for us all.

Debbie a member of the care staff had taken lots of photos of our day at the seaside, which I thought was lovely. A few days later, I saw the photos proudly displayed on the wall in the Main Hall, with a crowd of girls and staff remarking on them. "Don't I look good?", "I look better than you," and other polite and impolite comments. Then I heard "You don't look too bad either, Miss," from Sara, looking straight at me.

Horror of horrors, there I was in my swimsuit, even though I had specifically said "no photos of me please" and hidden myself away at every opportunity. "Oh, that's unexpected," I said, feeling more amused than annoyed and thinking to myself that in fact I did look quite good.

Another event was a concert being arranged for a Saturday evening. Parents, Foster parents, or Guardians were being invited as many of the girls were quite talented in their different ways. Sister Angela who was in charge of the proceedings, played the guitar and supplied accompaniment when necessary. Sisters Sonia and Natalie, as well as looking very attractive, were also accomplished guitar players and had quite good singing voices. The Teaching staff were not involved, but we provided lots of encouragement.

The evening of the concert in the Main Hall was packed with staff, girls, friends, and relatives of the performers. A stage decorated with flowers had been set up and we all now waited in anticipation. A hush fell on the crowd as Sister Angela swept onto the stage. She welcomed all the guests and invited everyone for a buffet supper after the show. I looked around the audience, recognising one or two members of the girl's families. I felt apprehensive, for as much as I wanted the girls to do well, I knew from experience this could never be guaranteed.

After a few words of introduction by Sister Angela each performance began. There was a poem to begin, followed by a sweet solo, a guitar solo, plus an amazing Rap by three of the girls. All went very well and each act was followed by rapturous applause.

Then came the performance I had been waiting for. The only two siblings at Ravenscourt at the moment were Sonia and Natalie. They came on to the stage. Such pretty girls, they had surpassed themselves in the outfit department, wearing dresses that they had obviously borrowed for the occasion, with a single flower in their hair. There was only a year's difference in their ages so they could have been twins. I was so busy looking at them I hadn't noticed they had started to play their guitars and sing. I felt that they would steal the show, whatever followed their act.

Again I was distracted as I began remembering the reason they were both in care. As it happened, the care worker I was sitting next to was involved with the family and she whispered to me "Those two are their Mum and Dad" she whispered, as she quietly pointed to a couple seated just in front of us. "The man in the red pullover is their Dad."

I didn't reply, but felt angry. I had thought he would still be in prison. At least there aren't any teenage boys with them, I thought with relief. For me, the rest of the evening passed in a daze as I wondered why on earth the girls would agree to their father being present. Or their mother for that matter, as she had been compliant with what had been going on. The evening came to an end. Everyone agreed it had been a great success.

Sonia and Natalie left Ravenscourt not long afterwards. Preparation had been in place for many months, with discussions amongst staff, both care and teaching that showed we were all anxious as to the future of these two girls, now approaching 18 and 17 years. Due to their very traumatic background extra vigilance would have to be put in place for them, and as it is very difficult for staff to keep in touch once a young person leaves care, as they sometimes move to a different area, and are catered for by a different set of Council workers. It was agreed in the case of Sonia and Natalie that staff were able to keep in contact. The girls were set up in a flat, found jobs and seemed to be doing alright. Sonia eventually married an older man, and Natalie settled down with a woman friend.

The position of Home Economics Teacher had been advertised, interviews had taken place and a new teacher appointed. The teaching staff hadn't been given any information beforehand, so we didn't know what to expect. We were told after the appointment, that the new member of staff was quite young, in her twenties and would be starting in September for the new term.

Sharon, for that was her name, fitted in with the team very quickly. She was a proficient teacher with a friendly caring attitude who shared problems with the group, was liked by the girls and staff and became "one of us" very quickly. She introduced the Duke of Edinburgh Award Scheme which was a big asset to the school, and she worked tirelessly to help some of the girls to achieve an award. All was well for a few years until she was "whisked away" by the man of her dreams, to travel the world!

CHAPTER NINE

All continued at a steady pace at Ravenscourt. The older girls were leaving and younger ones were arriving. There were problems of course, as in any set-up where large numbers of children lived, worked and played together, but these were dealt with in either the school or the home unit whenever they occurred. For the most part the girls worked well at their lessons and were rewarded with good results in the exams. Staff and girls enjoyed many excursions, as invitations continued to be received at this time. Also the BBC sent tickets for the filming of TV comedy shows with audience participation.

A Continuation of Care worker had been appointed as a liaison officer to cater for the needs of those leaving Ravenscourt. Averil was employed to work closely with the Social worker and the Local Authority, preparing a 'Pathway Plan' to decide what help and support to put in place, taking into account the age, needs and wants of the particular young person after they had left Care.

Averil worked very hard, keeping in touch with as many girls as possible after they had left Ravenscourt and from time to time organized Saturday gatherings for lunch. Many girls returned for this reunion, and often one or two brought their boyfriends, and all the new Mums brought their babies.

It was a delight to see them, although I felt sad that many of these girls, who were scarcely out of childhood themselves, were in such a hurry to have babies. Possibly neglected and sometimes abandoned in childhood they believed that a baby would solve their problems, and would always love them for the rest of their lives! Unfortunately, life is not always like that, but they weren't to know. I just hoped and prayed that life would be kind to these girls.

All was busy in the Staffroom one morning. As usual we arrived early, never quite knowing what was in store for us as we sorted ourselves out for the day ahead, whilst catching up on any personal news we had to share. This particular morning the door opened and Sister Mary and Sister Angela appeared and quietened us to say "We thought we would tell you now before you heard it from someone else. We will fill in all the details later" said Sister Mary. Then the blow fell. The Sisters were leaving! Their Order had recalled them. Five years had passed, and they had set up a successful Home and School. Now it was time to move on. It was the policy of the Order.

I felt the sunny morning had turned quite bleak, and looking around at the other teachers I could see that they were feeling the same way.

I pulled myself together, after all they were only people, and people could be replaced! Little did I know! I suddenly realised how much we had come to depend on the Sisters. The Head, Sister Mary was always around for support, never interfering but always available. Sister Angela Head of School, was highly efficient and caring and giving advice when needed. The three other Sisters involved in the work were caring and friendly, always willing to discuss individual girls if needed.

The second blow came when staff were told that senior members of the Care staff would be relocating also. These were highly experienced qualified people, both men and women, who excelled in their roles as 'loco parentis.' They had relocated with the Sisters for the setting up of Ravenscourt. We all looked at each other again, then back at the Sisters, then back at each other. We were a united group and as we had grown closer together over the five years, we each reflected the same feelings at the news. The unspoken question was how would this news affect our jobs, and would they still be secure? The Sisters had decided to give their news to individual groups separately. Most members of care staff already knew as they were on site. The girls would be told later.

Well, the day had to go on, lessons had to be taught, and we tried to keep things as normal as possible.

Later that day, the Sisters did fill us in as far as they could. They were not quite sure at that stage exactly what their future duties would be, but as far as the staff were concerned, that didn't include working with us. On the positive side we were assured that our jobs would be safe! New staff would have to be interviewed and appointed and that would take time, so all would remain as it was for some months.

On hearing the news of the departure of the sisters a number of the younger members of the care staff, perhaps afraid for their jobs under a new regime, and now uncertain of the future applied for other jobs. All members of the teaching staff decided to stick it to the bitter end.

During the following week I had a pleasant surprise when one of my first students at Ravenscourt telephoned me. Dana had refused to work for me at first, but turned out to be one of my best students. During her time at the school we had become quite close, as much as one can be with a student. She had often invited me over to the house for tea and biscuits.

Her news this time was very encouraging. She was now living in a flat near friends and family in Essex, and was working as a warden in Holloway, the women's prison. She was a strong well-built girl, with the sort of personality that would show the prisoners she would stand no nonsense. I was very pleased for her, but there was surprising, if not quite unexpected news to come. She had decided to stay working in the prison for a while, but was planning to attend College to train as a Social Worker. "I want to get somewhere, and become qualified, not getting bogged down with kids like some of me mates," she assured me. I knew she would do it as she was a bright girl and had worked hard at her lessons in Ravenscourt when she put her mind to it and she had obtained some qualifications already.

"I know it'll be a long time in the future, Miss, but will you recommend me?" she asked. I knew she meant provide a reference when the time was right, and of course I readily agreed. She had suffered a bad start in life and I would do all I could to help her to achieve success in the future. As we continued to chat she told me she was very happy with her life although she did not see much of her family, "and I ain't goin' to depend on that lot," she assured me. "My life is good, my friends are good, so I'm okay."

She gave me her address and telephone number and said she would like me to phone her sometime, which I did, and we had many such chats in the future. I put the phone down on that first occasion feeling quite uplifted that she had felt she could telephone me, and I was encouraged that Ravenscourt had helped her to build up her confidence and sense of self-worth to face the future.

One day during lunchtime as often happened, the teachers got together with members of the care staff for informal chats. Lesley who was a valued worker and was known for her selfless care for the girls confessed to having a problem. "I am at my wits end," she confided. "Due to a shortage of staff this evening, I really don't know what to do with Rosie. I can't give up another night due to family commitments." Knowing that Lesley had three children and a husband who worked shifts we all sympathised.

I hesitated, then made a suggestion. "I will have her for the night if you like?" Rosie had only been with us for a short time. She was a member of a Romany family. She was a delightful girl of 13 with dark curls and a quiet manner so I didn't think she would be any trouble. She had been taken into care for her own safety and protection.

Lesley's face lit up. "Would you really, you are a lifesaver."

Girls were not normally allowed to spend time with anyone at a moment's notice like this, but Lesley had visited my home and met my husband when coming to tea with girls before church on Sundays. I knew he would be quite happy with the arrangement, so it was agreed.

Driving home that afternoon Rosie said very little and not much about herself. "I like staying at people's houses," she said followed by "have you got a telly?" I brought the conversation around to food. "I'll eat anything," she assured me. Considering she had only met me four times in class she seemed very comfortable. I was the more nervous of the two!

Arriving home I showed her over the house including her room. She seemed quite happy. I explained to her that both my son and daughter were away at University, and often brought home friends to stay at the weekends at short notice so I always had beds prepared in the spare room. Lesley had instructed me to unobtrusively slip a black bin bag under the bottom sheet in case of accidents, so I had made a mental note to do just that.

Luckily I had prepared a casserole in the slow cooker that morning before leaving home, but I was not often so organized. Rosie laid the table, but her interest was in the telly. "You got the telly in a room by itself, why is that?" she asked. "Sometimes my husband works on his preparation or marking in the evening as he is a teacher too," I replied, "and I like watching telly."

I heard the front door shut and my husband appeared. He looked with surprise at Rosie, smiled in a friendly way and said "Hello, who do we have here?" I hadn't been able to warn him, but knew he would be fine with it. There were no mobiles in those days! We settled down to eat and all was going well as we chatted throughout the meal. Rosie talked about her brother and other members of her family in an abstract way as though they were nothing to do with her. I didn't ask any questions although I was longing to know more about her. She was quite happy to do most of the talking covering animals, school, etc. I felt quite happy that she seemed so much at home with us. She helped me to wash up and seemed very happy helping with mundane chores, which made me think she was used to it. When putting the plates and cutlery away she said "The knives and forks must go in the special gaps in the drawer, otherwise you'll get a hiding." I quickly changed the subject.

"Do you think your 'usband will do his writing work tonight?" she asked.

I replied "Yes, he probably will."

At her request we went out into the garden for a while. "I like flowers" she said, looking at what I saw to be a bunch of weeds. Then later a run of questions, "Can I have a shower now? Have you got a hairdryer?" she asked, and "Can I watch the telly then?"

So we went indoors. I led her to the bathroom and gave her all the necessary equipment and told her "I won't be far if you need me."

"I'll go to watch telly then, shall I?" she asked.

"Of course," I replied.

I went upstairs 20 minutes later to find her installed in front of the TV drying her hair. I knew she was used to spending time alone and her body language showed that she did not want company as she was sitting in the centre of the sofa, the only comfortable seating in the room. "I'll be in the kitchen doing some ironing if you need me," I told her.

She said she wanted to go to bed at 10 o'clock and mentioned "I like cocoa," so I took up a mug of it up for her. She had already changed into her pyjamas after her shower so was ready for bed. I tucked her in, said goodnight, and left the landing light on at her request.

The next morning she had cereal for breakfast. She was very pleased to be given a choice and settled for porridge which surprised me. I felt secretly that she wanted to see me actually making it as somehow it made her feel more cared for. I felt quite sad about it. She didn't say much but munched away happily asking for more toast and marmalade. There was just the two of us for breakfast as my husband was an early riser having quite a long journey to the college where he worked.

"Time to go, Rosie," I said. "We mustn't be late for school." We set off after locking up the house and Rosie watched this routine with interest. "We don't lock up our houses," she said. I wanted to ask her why not but as we were busy sorting ourselves out and putting bags into the boot of the car there wasn't any time.

The unexpected 'bed and breakfast' had gone without a hitch as far as I was concerned. On the way to school she said "I like staying with you and your 'usband miss, can I come again?"

I replied "Yes of course you can, we loved having you." Unfortunately it did not happen as Rosie was shortly moved to a Children's Home nearer to her family.

CHAPTER TEN

During the month or so that followed, life at Ravenscourt appeared to be going along as normal, but there was an undercurrent of tension that showed itself both in the staff and the girls. They felt insecure as yet more people were leaving their lives. The sisters had given an air of permanence, perhaps it was the habit they wore? The girls asked teaching staff from time to time "You aren't leaving as well are you, Miss?"

One day I had a surprise invitation from Shelley. A surprise because she was a girl I did not see very much of. I knew cooking was her favourite subject, and in the Home Economics lessons, girls were encouraged to cook for others. "Would you and Bren like to come to supper with me next week?" she asked. I said of course I would be delighted, and didn't point out that she had my husband's name wrong. She had never met Bryn, but it seemed that word had gone round from the girls who had visited my home on a Sunday, that he was a friendly chap! A date was chosen and it was all arranged. I checked on the quiet with Shelley's House Mother, who said that she was in on it and would be in the background helping.

The day of the supper arrived. We had chosen our outfits for the evening with care. Not knowing what to take, I had chosen a small posy of mixed flowers. On arrival I was puzzled as to where we would be entertained. I had visited the unit many times, but surely we wouldn't be entertained in the large dining room, the centre of which was an oak table seating twelve, or alternately in the Living Room, where the other girls would be sitting, reading or watching TV. I need not have worried. At the top of the stairs Shelley appeared. She had been watching out for us, which I thought was quite sweet. I introduced them.

"This is my husband, Bryn," I said, and Shelley replied "Oh yes, I don't know you but I've heard about you."

He gave the usual reply "All good I hope?"

"Oh yes," she replied, "I've heard you're nice."

She led us into a small room to the left of the dining room. I hadn't realised its existence. It was a cosy room, and in the corner was a small table, just big enough for three or four people. It was neatly laid for supper with cutlery, water jug and glasses, and pretty paper napkins. The room also contained a small sofa, a desk and bookcase. It was obvious that the room belonged to a member of care staff who had lent it out for the evening.

I was very touched that such a lot of work had gone into preparations for this evening. There was a space in the middle for my posy which was in a tiny glass bowl. I had presented the posy to Shelley on arrival but she did not take it from me. She blushed pink and said "That's nice." She was not used to receiving flowers I thought.

I said tentatively "Shall I put the flowers in the middle of the table, what do you think?"

She replied shyly. "Yes that would be nice."

She showed us to our seats and said "Won't be long," reappearing minutes later accompanied by her Key worker. She pointed to Karen saying "She's helping me, but I cooked." The meal was delicious, a lasagne followed by a chocolate pudding. Not much was said during the meal; we complimented Shelley on the meal and kept up small talk, mostly about school. I knew very little about her background except that she had been put into care for her own protection. She did not mention anything about her family and of course neither did we. I felt the whole situation was very comfortable. She looked after us with the air of a professional hostess. We felt at home with her and her with us. It was a lovely evening. We stayed at the table, she plying us with seconds and more of the excellent fruit drink that had appeared on the table. We could hear the sounds coming from the Living area, but due to the structure of the very old building, the sound was muffled. No-one disturbed us so they had obviously been told that it was Shelley's evening and they were to respect that. At ten o'clock I thought it was time to take our leave. We thanked Shelley for a lovely evening. She had appeared comfortable in our company and accompanied us to the top of the stairs leading to the ground floor. Not knowing quite what to do by way of leaving. I would give a hug to friends at this point, but I left it to her to take the initiative. She put out her hand for Bryn to shake, then turned to me and gave a brief hug. I was very touched. She was a fifteen year old girl, with such confidence and poise in one so young. I felt tears in my eyes as on the way home I was thinking about the evening. I prayed that whatever the future held for Shelley, that she would excel at what she did and that life would be good to her. Whenever I thought about the evening, or confided to friends about it, I always felt moved to tears.

During the next few weeks, there was a lot of activity. The Sisters usually spent quite a bit of time in their own home, which was a comfortable little house two or three miles from Ravenscourt. Now they were appearing oftener. We knew something was up. Whether or not the Care staff knew any more than we did, the teaching staff were told very little of what was going on. It was obvious to us that interviews were taking place in Sister Mary's rooms, which consisted of a study and ante-rooms on the third floor.

We were finally told that a Head of Ravenscourt had been appointed. His name was Robert Williams and that he had a wealth of experience in leading teams of workers in Residential Care Homes. I wondered what it would be like, a man replacing Sister Mary. Quite different I should think. Williams is a good old Welsh name, so I felt hopeful.

Then came the news the Teaching staff had been waiting for. A Head of Education had been appointed and we were to meet her the following day. Who could replace the gentle Sister Angela with her firm yet caring guidance, always being there but never interfering? It was with fear and trepidation that I faced the woman who would be our new boss. Veronica was a small woman who looked to be in her thirties. She smiled at us with confidence. I would describe her as small, yet with a presence that seemed to convey that she would be 'an authority, in authority'. She said "I have had vast experience in dealing with this kind of girl." I didn't care for the way she put it, but told myself I was just being picky. Discussing her afterwards, we all agreed that she was likeable, friendly and obviously capable of doing the job!

Replacement Care staff had also been appointed but we were only able to find out who they were when they began work.

It was a Friday afternoon, the end of the working week. As usual there was a treat laid out in the Teachers staffroom that we all looked forward to each week. This treat was courtesy of the local Marks and Spencer store. Boxes containing packs of fresh fruit, vegetables and many items of chilled cooked meals, such as packs of lasagne and pies arrived. There must have been mountains of goodies delivered to the premises, as of course the units had the first choice, and teenage girls have big appetites. The staff had the remainder, which was quite considerable. "Good old M&S," we quipped, as we helped ourselves; there was always plenty to go round. We were not to know that these treats were to be discontinued when the Sisters left.

The Sisters were packing up their belongings. Their beloved Chapel, the room they had fashioned from scratch at the very beginning, would have originally been a small study, sitting-room, or even a downstairs bedroom of the old house. The walls were oak panelled, lovely mullion windows overlooked the grounds; it contained a beautiful enormous stone fireplace, and the lovely red carpet the Sisters had chosen. The room was now stripped of all the Religious statues and wall hangings, also the lovely pine table where the Priest celebrated the Eucharist was to go. This table had been specially hand made for the Sisters when they fashioned the room into a Chapel. Light in weight, it had cut-outs on the sides and base which was a reminder of the shape of Church stained glass windows.

I was passing the Chapel at lunchtime, noticing the Sisters moving things around ready for transportation. The life-size statue of the Founder of their Order was missing from the hallway leading to the chapel. The statue had been greatly revered, strangely even by those who did not believe in 'idols' such as myself, so now it really sunk in that things would never be the same again! Looking up from packing books into a box Sister Mary called me inside. "I thought perhaps you would like the table on which we celebrate the Mass," she said. She was supported in this plan by the other Sisters who nodded with smiling faces. I was overcome with emotion at such a generous offer, and as a Christian I was doubly excited. "How wonderful," I gasped, "it will always remind me of you Sisters and our lives at Ravenscourt."

"Can you take it now?" said Sister Mary.

"You bet," I thought but actually said "Yes, thank you." I managed to get it into the car, seeing no-one on the way. It seems strange to me now, but I didn't tell anyone on the staff of the generous gift I had received. This table has been precious to me ever since, and is now standing proudly in my conservatory holding plants in pots.

The teaching staff along with key members of Care staff had been trying to decide how we could give the Sisters a suitable send-off. We felt that to do this successfully, we needed to celebrate somewhere off site. A restaurant was out of the question. We called a secret meeting to discuss our plans. Mary-Anne bounced in, she had got there before us in her planning and had come up with the perfect solution. "Would you all like to come to my house for a meal?" she suggested. "It's not a big house, but we've a 2 acre garden so I thought a Marquee would be nice. I've got all the arrangements in mind, so you lot have only to agree, and I'll get on with it." We readily agreed, and thanked her for her kindness. We knew that her partner was a millionaire, but that does not always make for generosity. We offered help but was assured she would have everything planned. We just had to turn up. She sent out invitations and we all looked forward to the evening.

Mary-Ann had been going around with a secretive look, not letting on about any of her arrangements for the send-off evening at her house. All she said was "Put on your posh frocks, long if possible, and the men should wear DJ's if possible or their best suit!"

The big night arrived. It was the end of July and a beautiful evening. 'Just as well if we were going to eat in a tent' I thought. We all arrived at roughly the same time. We had been told "7 for 7.30." We were dropped off in various way, some by their partners, a friend or by taxi. We weren't going to drive in our posh frocks.

Walking down the drive from the gate, we were met by a sight only seen in the movies. There was Mary-Ann looking splendid in a striped grey and white silk ball gown. She was standing in the entrance to the Tent, which consisted of a wonderful creation covered in white silk. There were lit torches all around the grounds, with small tables laden with drinks of all kinds plus glasses, and each table decorated with flowers. After greeting us Mary-Ann gestured to the tables. Just as if by magic, waiters appeared to serve us. When we had all arrived we were led into the Marquee. We gasped in wonder at the sight. The white and gold silk hangings were decorated with dozens of white balloons, the long table was laid for the meal in the usual way with glasses and cutlery. Down the centre of the table the gold and white flowers looked amazing and were set off by dozens of lighted white candles. There was around twenty of us. Every one of the Teachers had been invited, plus all the Leading Care workers, and of course the Sisters as this was their send-off evening. The Head, Sister Mary had decided not to come. She must have given her apologies to Mary-Ann, but I was sure at the time that she was with us in spirit! The Sisters were dressed in their 'civvies', looking very glamorous, though very well covered up of course, unlike the rest of us women. There were only two men present, both were Key Care workers, but they didn't seem at all inhibited by all the ladies, as in fact they seemed to delight in being in the minority.

It was a six course meal, served by smartly dressed waiters. Sister Angela said Grace and the meal began. We were served Soup, fish, main course, sorbet, sweet and cheese. There were wines complimenting each course, followed by coffee and liqueurs. Drink driving was not as strict in the 80s, but it was a good thing we all had lifts home. At the end of what was a wonderful evening, Mary-Ann presented us all with a small gift. My gift was a silver bookmark, but what was even more touching was the little note she placed inside the box. I have never used the bookmark, as I was fearful of it getting lost. I still look at it from time to time, and when I read the flattering comments contained in the little note, I ask myself 'Am I really that person?' We were all overcome by the generosity of Mary-Ann.

The end of term approached. We all said our farewells to the Sisters. I knew I would never forget this particular and most memorable time in my teaching experience. I would never forget the girls who had left and looked forward to seeing the girls who remained with us in the next school year in September. My experience of working with the Sisters was a unique one. Their way of working, combining a strict regime with a caring and friendly attitude, with high expectations was a way to be envied. The staff and girls had great respect for them, and also great affection. My lasting memory of Sister Mary would always be the look on her face as she came into the staffroom holding up a photograph. 'What had she been up to,' I wondered. The Sisters always kept their private lives 'private'. I knew they were women of great faith, and spent much time in Prayer and Supplication, but their 'off time' was a bit of a mystery.

All was revealed; Sister Mary had visited Rome and had been lucky enough (or was it through prayer?) to gain an audience with Pope John Paul II. The photograph was living proof of their meeting as we saw Sister Mary bowing slightly over his hand. He was quite special, as being Polish, he was the first non-Italian Pope in over 400 years.

CHAPTER ELEVEN

The term was drawing to a close. Care staff and Social workers were busy sorting out holiday arrangements for the girls. Many would be remaining at Ravenscourt for at least part of the time. If home circumstances permitted, a girl would spend part of the time with her family, closely supervised by her Social Worker.

Foster Carers, those known to a girl, would have her to stay for a given period of time. Stacy, whose mother had refused to have her home for weekends had now relented, allowing her home for part of the holiday.

Reports by Social workers and other key figures, along with the obvious improvement in her daughter's attitude and behaviour had softened the heart of the mother, who still insisted "this will still be a trial period."

Stacy was thrilled and promised to be "The changed daughter." She had been working hard at her lessons and had passed several examinations. "Wait till me mum sees this on paper," she said proudly.

We on the staff wondered what to expect in September, as the new Head of Ravenscourt and the new Head of Education took their places amongst us. 'Thank goodness for the Teaching staff,' I thought, at least we are all returning. We had formed a strong group, and most of us had been together for the five years since the Home had opened.

The summer holidays had begun. There was not much time for dwelling on what the new term would bring! I had looked forward to the long break. That particular year my husband and I were spending three weeks touring France, ending up in the South for a week, and visiting friends in Nice, who had moved there to set up a church.

The six weeks went by quickly. Soon it was time to think about the new autumn term, including the planning of lessons. When returning to school after a holiday break, none of us knew quite what to expect. We were 'teachers' of the girls, and though quite involved to a certain extent we had no say in the planning or organising of their future, unless it concerned their academic abilities. It was quite likely that decisions had been made for a girl, and she would have 'moved on,' to another Care placement, nearer home, or arrangements had been made for her to leave school if she was of leaving age.

Possibly there would be new students in place, ready to start the school term. Coupled with the forthcoming new Leadership regime there was much to think about! What was going to happen, what changes could we expect, how would the changes affect the girls?

PART TWO

CHAPTER TWELVE

Autumn had arrived, and nothing could stop it, in spite of the fact that the weather was still quite warm and sunny, with no early morning frost which signals the beginning of the end of the year. Autumn term had begun, and with it a new school year. 'What was it to bring?' I wondered. We all arrived early in the Teachers staffroom. Early arrival was usual after a long break.

We greeted each other with the usual "How was your holiday?", "What did you get up to?", "Any pics?" There was so many of these, that we decided to leave the showing of them until lunchtime. We had all had a good holiday and a much needed break. No major catastrophes had occurred, so we all shared the hope that the new term would be a good one!

"Let's hope that the new 'bosses' will fit in," said Janet, who sometimes said out loud what the rest of us were thinking!

"Hope so," we all echoed.

Veronica, the New Head of Education, came quietly into the room. "Good morning all," she said. "Very glad you are all early, so we can have a bit of a chat." We all sat down in our usual chairs, while she kept standing, even though there was a spare chair she could have sat on. 'Was her body language making a statement?' I wondered. To be fair, she was quite a small person, so maybe she would have felt that her superiority would not be evident if she was on a level with the rest of us! Who knows!

I had expected that the staff would have been called in for a meeting on a day before term began. This would have been a more professional approach to her duties as Head. All we were getting was a brief chat before the beginning of the term. She said very little, giving nothing away about her Aims and Objectives, or how she saw her role. All would be revealed in due time it seems. She informed us that she would be taking an Assembly in the Main Hall, each morning at 9.15 a.m. Mr Williams, the newly appointed Head of Ravenscourt, would be present on the first morning, but unlike Sister Mary his predecessor, he would not be a regular attendant, as we soon found out. We never got the chance to use his Christian name, which was Robert. 'Bob' would have been friendly, but from the beginning we were encouraged to always use 'Mr'.

The teaching staff entered the Hall to a surprising sight. The girls accompanied by Care staff were already in their seats. The girls were sitting together, which was unusual, perhaps they gained comfort from one another as they faced the new regime. The girls who were familiar with the teachers, having been in the school longer, gave a smile and a wave as we went in. After a few minutes the new Head of Ravenscourt accompanied by the Head of Education came in together. They sat on the two empty seats which had been set out for them. Mr Williams introduced himself. This was the first time many of the girls had seen him. Veronica had visited the units and introduced herself to them the day before, when they had arrived after the holidays. She reintroduced herself. Assembly was a very casual affair with no structure, as Veronica talked generally about matters that concerned both the units and the school. This meeting lasted a short while and we were dismissed to go to our classes. I don't think I was the only one to miss the structure and Spiritual input we had received from the Sisters. I chided myself, whatever my feelings were I must be prepared for change. We must move on, I thought. Veronica had made it clear that assembly would not contain any Spiritual element.

School carried on in much the same way, as the girls settled down in the new term. To my surprise they didn't say much about the new members of staff apart from "They seem alright," "They're not too bad I s'pose." They were used to so much change in their young lives that they took it in their stride. I was determined to do all I could to make their time in school happy and fruitful. Stacey returned to school very happy. Her time at home with her mum had been very successful, and when the time came for her to leave school for good, she would be welcomed home. Little by little over the next week, some of the girls confided to me what their holiday period had been like. Sian was in a negative mood. Not a lot had happened during the holiday as she had spent most of the time in Ravenscourt. I did not press her, she would tell me in her own time what the problem was! The other girls reported positive and negative happenings that had taken place during the holiday period. Quite natural happenings in the lives of teenagers, as I remember with my own children, and even as far back as my own teenage years! My sister and I had a very happy childhood, but I would be the first to say I was not an easy teenager!

There were three new girls who had been put into the care system, and The Local Authority had decided Ravenscourt was suitable for them. They were all very young, thirteen and fourteen. I was pleased to see that some of the older girls were protective of them, and took them under their wing. The teachers would learn more from the girls themselves, as they gained trust and confidence in the adults around them, and shared some of their experiences. This was usually done in a casual and offhand way, as this was their way of communicating. I felt highly privileged when they shared their past experiences with me. I've never forgotten the time when one of the girls, a quiet solitary girl said, "I've been thrown down stairs sixteen times you know, Miss, and broken lots of bones." I didn't know whether or not to believe her, as I found it so difficult to imagine, but the only words I could say was "I'm so sorry, poor you." I held my breath, wondering where this was going, but luckily this answer seemed to satisfy her. She just smiled shyly and said "Thanks."

There did not seem to be many changes taking place, at least not in the school. There was a number of new Care Staff who all seemed very capable and were liked by the girls. Veronica held a teachers staff meeting each Friday. She seemed satisfied with the work we were doing in the classrooms. No new ideas or thoughts were introduced to begin with. She did not spend as much time with us as the previous head had done. Sister Angela had always been in and out of the staffroom, and indeed even though she was the boss she seemed 'one of us'. We hardly ever saw Mr Williams as he spent a lot of his time in his office, whereas Sister Mary had always been around the place, popping into the teachers' staff room or spending time in the units.

Veronica fitted in with the staff and we became used to her. We were a close supportive group of teachers, who were able to deal with any matter that arose with the confidence that only a united group brings.

Autumn Half term arrived. Veronica was settling in her new job as Head of Education. No obvious changes had taken place, apart from Assembly which had turned into a casual 'happening'. The gathering together at the beginning of the day was causing the girls to be restless whereas previously, assembly had been a well-structured time which interested and settled everyone for the day ahead. Mr Williams the Head of Ravenscourt was conspicuous by his absence as he spent most of his time in his third floor office. Lessons carried on as usual with the girls working at their own pace, some very well, some not so well which was to be expected. Several of the older girls would be leaving at the end of term, so preparations were being made as Key workers, Social workers, and the Local Authority worked together to enable a satisfactory transition to be made for each girl.

Half term arrived, and we were all looking forward to the break. I felt it had been a fairly successful early part of the term. Most of the girls had worked quite well in class and seemed quite happy, as nothing had changed as far as school was concerned.

School resumed after the half-term holiday. Classes were smaller as several older girls had left school. Stacy was due to leave, but things had not gone to plan, so she would remain here for another few weeks. As her tutor I expected to be informed in due course of what was going on. She did not seem to know anything definite at this stage. I thought that her mum was probably at the centre of the problem, but it was not my place to say anything.

Teaching staff meetings were held Friday lunchtimes. Veronica had news for us in that she had appointed a new teacher who was to be the new Art teacher. There was a gap in the teaching programme as a number of teachers had begun work with us, but none had lasted very long. Judy our Maths teacher also taught art and this worked very well, but a new Art teacher would be very welcome. Sofie, for that was her name, would be starting work after the Christmas break.

With Christmas fast approaching I was determined to celebrate it in the way I thought it should be celebrated. The chapel was never used, so I decided to hold a service for the staff and girls. But first I had to seek permission from Veronica She could not refuse such a request surely. Numbers of students were down at the moment, as there had been no replacements yet for the girls who had left. Small though the chapel was, we should be able to get in enough chairs for everyone, as there was no furniture. I decided not to mention this plan to anyone for the moment.

But Veronica got in before me. At the meeting on Friday she outlined her plans for the New Year. One of them concerned me. "I have decided to move you from your present classroom into the Chapel. It is not being used now, and I want your classroom for our new Art Teacher." I was aghast. The staff room was very stuffy, with three smokers in the room, who were adverse to open windows, so to give myself a moment I got up. "It's very smokey in here" I said, and threw open two of the long windows. Normally at least one of the smokers would have said "Oh you and your fresh air," but this time not a word was uttered.

I loved the Chapel, but did not see it as a possible classroom. True, numbers were down at the moment, but surely new girls would be joining us? In the beginning I had been given one of the biggest classrooms. It was lovely room overlooking the grounds, with lots of room for store cupboards, tables, and later on space for five PC's. I pointed this out to her, as I showed my annoyance. "I need your classroom for my new Art teacher." She announced in her no argument voice. I tried to feel positive. The Chapel was in the front of the building after all, with a lovely window, small, but still overlooking the grounds through the little panes. "It's my decision," she said again. I could not argue, she was the in charge person. How I longed for the return of Sister Angela.

I then changed the subject and put my Christmas Service plan in front of her. The other teachers nodded in agreement. Veronica did not say much, she just agreed, and a date was set. I put the idea to the girls. Just as I had expected, three of the older girls showed an interest. They were familiar with me, and felt confident in joining in with my plan. "We'll help you, Miss," they chorused. The younger girls were comparative newcomers to Ravenscourt but assured me they would join in the singing of Carols. I planned a meeting with Tracy, Sian and Michelle. Tracy was to give a short introduction to each presentation, Michelle would read a short Bible verse, and Sian would read a Christmas poem. Hopefully the rest of the service would fall into place. I discussed the event with other members of the Teaching staff, and Janet offered to show everyone to their seats, the others offering help as and when needed. I just needed to get on with the work needed to complete my plan. A lot of typing and photocopying would be needed.

Looking around the Chapel objectively for the first time since I was told it was to be my new classroom, I felt a sudden warmth come over me. I had always felt that the Chapel held a certain warmth, and had put that down to the presence of the Sisters, but I now felt that the warmth had been retained, perhaps in the walls, or was it something else? Feeling happy and positive I tried to imagine what my chairs, tables and PC's would look like, and asked myself, where on earth would the Stationery cupboard go?

Moving on to more pressing matters, I started to plan the Christmas decorations for the room ready for the service. Chairs from the Main hall were to be brought in, and I planned to put a small Christmas tree in the vast fireplace. Even though the Christmas tree is a pagan symbol, introduced to this country by Prince Albert, I thought it would be a jolly addition to the festivities, and when consulted on the decorations, the first question from the girls was "How big is the Christmas tree going to be?" I would be bringing all the decorations from home, and using fresh greenery from the garden, with permission from Jim the gardener of course. Feeling more positive, I returned to my daily duties.

The day of the Christmas Concert arrived. I looked

around the Chapel with satisfaction at the tree and the decorations. The chairs had been put in place by Jim and his helpers. I didn't count them but the number looked OK. The Christmas cards I had received looked festive on the mantelpiece of the grand fireplace. The door opened and a voice called out, "Here we are." and in came Stacy, Sian and Michelle right on time, clutching their respective 'party pieces', ready for a quick run through. All went according to plan. They were word perfect, and glowed under the praise I showered upon them. Jenny was to hand out the Order of service, so she arrived early. They were all carefully dressed, each sporting an item of clothing in red or green, and in Tracy's case both. I felt touched that they had taken so much trouble. Each girl had a tiny Christmas decoration on her jumper, or in Michelle's case, in her hair.

Everyone began to arrive and were shown to their seats and given a Service sheet. Each girl was accompanied by either her key worker or another member of staff, some of whom were strangers to me, as many of the main Care workers had left and were being replaced by new recruits. The teachers were already seated. The room was packed as everyone had arrived. I noticed my husband had crept in and was standing at the back as there were no spare seats. He had promised me he would try and take the time off College to attend my little function. I was very pleased to see Jim standing next to him, and felt touched that he had decided to come. Clare, a long-standing member of the Care staff, and very musical took her place at the piano, which had been brought in from the Hall.

I welcomed everyone and thanked them for coming. Stacy stepped shyly forward and introduced the first Carol which was 'Away in a Manger'. This was followed by Michelle telling the Birth of Jesus story, reading from the Gospel of Luke, Chapter 2:vs1-7. We sang another carol Hark the Herald Angels sing followed by Sian reading a lovely Christmas poem 'A Prayer at Christmas,' by John Kennedy, taken from his book 'I'm Wond'ring'. I could see that many were touched by the beautiful words contained in this prayer/poem as they wiped tears from their eyes. They were also touched that Sian with all her problems/demons, could read out a poem such as this was, with the feeling the writer intended. The final Carol, The Holly and the Ivy, chosen by the girls during our rehearsal ended our service, was sung with gusto, followed by a thank you for coming from Stacy. A loud applause broke out, directed at the three girls who took part, who were now standing in a row together near the fireplace. Everyone filed out, thanking me for an enjoyable start to the Christmas Festivities, but it was the three girls who really made the beginning of the Christmas season special for me. I was quite overcome as I thanked and praised them later.

The term came to an end. I wondered what my "Chapel classroom", as I had come to think of it, would look like on my return. I had put my suggestions to Veronica, as to my preferences for layout and positioning of the desks, cupboard and equipment, but had been brushed aside with "all that is in hand, and will be fine by the time you return." I couldn't say that I was reassured, but as I had other more pressing matters to think about, I put it out of my mind.

It was a special Christmas for us that year. Our son and daughter-in-law had become parents to Daniel, a lovely baby boy, and it was to be his first Christmas. It was our first time as grandparents, so we were very excited. My daughter and son-in-law had invited the whole family to visit them in Birmingham for Christmas. There was lots of presents to buy as usual, but this year our shopping trips included a number of visits to Toys R Us.

CHAPTER THIRTEEN

I returned to school looking forward to what the new school year would bring. Returning early, the first thing I did was to visit my new classroom. The heavy iron key was still in the lock as usual, so in a strange way, this was reassuring. On opening the door I met a pleasant sight. The room looked good, as all the desks and chairs were in the best possible position, the stationary cupboard did not overpower the room as I had feared. The focal point was still the fireplace, which seemed to stand out in elegance. Just inside stood an amazing pottery jug, obviously very old, and probably one half of the set of Jug and washbasin that was used many years ago in the Grand House. I made a mental note; first thing I would do was to buy ornamental grasses to fill the jug. Little did I think that one day in the not too distant future, this jug would end up in my conservatory at home. The red carpet looked great. It was a good start to the year I thought.

I entered the teachers' staffroom, the last to arrive as I had taken longer than I had intended, in my new classroom. We all greeted each other, but there was no time for pleasantries at that stage. We would all catch up later. Veronica was holding forth, as she seemed to be holding a mini-meeting. She introduced the new Art teacher to me, as she had already met the others. Sofie looked to be in her thirties, and was pleasant and friendly.

The term began. The girls seemed pleased with the new classroom, but in their usual laid-back way decided not to say anything much about it. The view from the window was still good, showing the sweeping lawns, but somewhat limited, as the windows were smaller, but that was just as well, as there was nothing to cause a distraction. Veronica did not ask me at any point what I thought of the room.

The pattern of Assembly remained the same, just the meeting together of the Care staff, Teachers and girls for a talk by Veronica the Head of school, then sending off to classrooms. We were now used to this format and accepted it as the 'norm.' The Principal Mr Williams did not appear at any of these gatherings.

A number of replacement Care staff was now in place. They were all pleasant and friendly, and the girls had already formed good relationships with them. I hoped that the new Care workers would be as conscientious as the previous ones had been, in encouraging the girls in their school work as well as their numerous responsibilities as 'loco parentis.' As numbers were down, hopefully, further girls would be referred by the Local Authority to replace them.

The term progressed without any major catastrophes and school carried on without too many changes. The girls worked quite well at all subjects, behaviour was acceptable most of the time. The new Art teacher had settled in well and was liked by all. She worked hard and encouraged everyone to have a go at drawing and painting. The teachers had a go and I actually managed to produce a water colour of a jar of flowers. I thought it was rubbish, but Sofie praised it as a good first effort. She was just being kind. Many girls produced good work, and were justifiable proud. The Art room was soon covered in colourful watercolours and sketches. She had certainly got the girls going. One such painting hung proudly in my classroom, as it had been presented to me as a gift by Stacy.

Invitations to the BBC and London theatres seemed to have dried up for the present, but hopefully would be resumed sometime. The calm presence of the Sisters was missed by staff and girls alike. The space near the window in the main corridor where the life-size statue of the founder of the Order had stood looked strangely bare, and seemed to cry out for a table with a plant on it, which was silly, as it had seemed invisible to those of us who had passed it several times a day. It had seemed to generate a sort of calm.

There were subtle changes taking place under our very noses which did not register at the time. In school our main concern was the welfare and well-being of the girls, their learning, and helping to build up their self-esteem. Discipline was proving a bit more difficult than previously. A number of the older girls had reached leaving age. A gap had been left, as some of these girls had been good role models for the younger ones, being used as they were to the disciplined and more organised approach of the Sisters.

Concern was being shown among members of the Care staff, as the Teachers were unofficially told that a girl had been caught climbing over the wall at night to meet a boy in the town.

Community meetings were no longer held. This was a Community children's home, but no longer felt like it. School was kept separate, and Teachers were kept in the dark to the 'goings-on' outside the classroom. Looking back, I saw that Community meetings had been a big asset to all concerned, although they had been painful at the time to everyone concerned. With hindsight I felt that these meetings had greatly benefited the girls concerned. The new Head of School obviously felt that what went on in the Units was of no concern to the Teachers. This was quite alien to what had been happening over the past five and a half years, and took a bit of getting used to. In fact I never did get used to it.

Family meetings had always taken place on site. I was therefore very surprised when as Stacy's tutor, I was summoned to attend a meeting at a Social Services office in Essex. I very much hoped that this would be the final meeting, and Stacy's mum would allow her to return home. She was now 17 and had dismissed any idea of moving into a Council property, which would have been provided for her if she so desired. Home was the only item on her agenda.

We started off bright and early that Wednesday morning, as it was going to be a long journey. A car was laid on with the Social worker at the wheel and Stacy in the front passenger seat. I climbed into the back seat and was confronted by the only other passenger. She was a young girl. Who was she I wondered, and where was Stacy's Key worker? As no introductions were forthcoming, I thought it only polite to introduce myself. "I'm Stacy's tutor," I said. "I don't think we have met before," all the while taking in the girl's demeanour and appearance. She was young and pretty, wearing a very short skirt, and her nails were painted a bright red.

To my complete surprise she answered brightly. "I'm Anna, Stacy's new Key worker." Still reeling from the shock, I hoped my face did not reflect what I was feeling at that moment. To my great relief I didn't have to reply, as she prattled on. "I'm new, I didn't think I'd get the job, as I'm not qualified or anything." It was not usual for me to be short of words, but I was stuck for anything to say. As hard as I tried not to, my face must have betrayed something of my inner feelings.

"I'm nineteen," she said, somewhat defiantly, as if

nineteen was a completely acceptable age to work in a Key position with a vulnerable troubled girl, who had so much baggage.

Was this a sign of things to come, I asked myself cynically, that all new employees had to be young and inexperienced as well as unqualified? What was the Management thinking when they employed a girl such as Anna to help care for vulnerable troubled girls? I pulled myself together. It was not Anna's fault. My concern was for Stacy. Had she heard any of this conversation? With relief I saw that she had her Walkman firmly clamped to her ears, and was quietly humming to whatever tune she was listening to. I wondered what on earth Anna could contribute to the meeting. She was a talker that's for sure, and like all teenagers she liked talking about herself. She continued chatting, and I hoped I was making the appropriate responses.

The Family meeting followed the usual pattern except for the venue. Instead of sitting in a circle looking out at a view of lawns and trees, which looked great even in bad weather, we all alighted from the car, entered the rather gloomy building and shuffled up the narrow stairs in the Social Services offices. We then crammed into a small stuffy room, and I noticed that all windows were shut. Did I dare to ask for them to be opened? I decided No, for the moment. Mum was waiting, accompanied by a member of the Social Services team. I glanced at Stacy, who looked apprehensive, possibly waiting for Mum to make the first move, possibly to get up and give her a hug. This was not forthcoming, Stacy looked disappointed, but I did not take this lack of overt affection to mean anything. It was evident from previous meetings, that Mum loved her daughter and wanted to be reunited with her permanently at some point, but understandably, due to her daughter's past misdemeanours was nervous and hesitant. We'll see I thought.

The meeting was successful up to a point. The reports given by all were positive. I was able to truthfully report that Stacy had always been a very good student. She had passed her RSA Elementary and Intermediate Word Processing exams. She was a very bright girl. She was looking forward to applying for a job in an office. This impressed Mum, and I was hopeful for a successful outcome. Not quite what I had hoped for. Mum said she was very happy with the way her wayward daughter had matured and "become clever" as she put it. She would now have her home for good, but she refused to name a date. "Near future," was all she would agree to. We returned to Ravenscourt with Stacy a bit downcast, but with positive encouraging noises from the Social worker and me, she cheered up. Little did I think that one day in the future I would be invited to visit Stacy and Mum at their home. On the day I visited, which was a year or so later, the next door neighbour was also there for tea, and I was called Stacy's old teacher when Mum introduced me, seemingly very proud that 'teacher' was visiting. "Not so much the old," I said jokingly, and we all laughed. By this time, Stacy had a regular boyfriend and she was proudly pregnant. "You'll have to come again when the baby is born," I was told. I thought that this was just words, but in fact I was invited when Stacy gave birth to a lovely baby boy.

After a very successful five days at an Outward Bound Centre in Wales, there was nothing further planned for the girls. Summer had arrived and with it, some sunny weather. A trip to the seaside could be planned maybe. It was not in the hands of the Teachers to plan, so we had to wait and see if anything would be arranged.

A visit to our Church on the following Sunday brought an unexpected invitation. Sheena and Trevor who were members, lived in a prestigious gated housing estate. Members of the Church had been invited to use their grounds, which included a great outdoor swimming pool, complete with changing rooms, where we had held a number of BBQ's and other parties. Knowing of my work with teenage girls, we were invited for an afternoon of swimming at the pool. I was delighted and as the weather forecast had been good for the following ten days, a date was set. I had to obtain permission from the Head, but that should not be a problem.

The girls were very pleased to receive the invitation. They loved swimming and we were regular visitors to the local indoor pool, but this was something different. Someone had invited them to their home for a swim.

After a short journey, we arrived at the gated estate,

where comments such as "How posh," "Are your friends very rich?" "Do we have to pay to go in?" were uttered. "It's like the movies," said one. Sheena was waiting for us, and greeted us in her relaxed friendly way. The girls looked in awe at the two acre garden where the swimming pool stood out in splendour looking like a movie set. I knew the girls would behave themselves. They visibly relaxed and entered the changing rooms amidst whoops of joy and laughter. I also relaxed and got my camera ready to record the afternoon. I did not swim but chose instead to supervise the proceedings. I need not have worried, as the girls organised themselves and enjoyed the whole experience. Sheena very sensibly left us to it, as she thought the girls would be more relaxed without the presence of someone they were not familiar with.

I thought the afternoon had come to an end, as the girls all neatly dressed with hair combed, and in some cases, a dash of lipstick on, towels and wet cossies rolled up under arms, prepared to leave. Sheena came out of the house, as we prepared to say our farewells and thanks you's for a lovely afternoon. To our surprise she said "Do come into the house, I've got a cup of tea ready for you all." The girls had lost all shyness that they sometimes displayed with strangers, and seemed keen to agree. We trouped in to see a table laid for tea with sandwiches and a lovely chocolate cake taking pride of place. I was very grateful to Sheena. How kind of her I thought, to round off the afternoon in this way. We sat down in the chairs provided and the food was handed round.

A little voice piped up "I don't like tea, can I have water, please?" Sharon, the youngest member of the group, had only been at Ravenscourt for a short time.

"Sorry, I didn't think," said Sheena. "How many of you would like a coke instead?" Having two teenage sons, there was bound to be plenty of coke in the fridge. All hands shot up, so there was coke for all. Two teas only were on order, for Sheena and me.

We returned to the unit after a lovely afternoon, and there was much that the girls had to report to Care staff, that they started as soon as they stepped through the door. The experience was a topic of conversation for days, and the girls surprised and pleased to report that they had all received an invitation to visit again the following week.

CHAPTER FOURTEEN

One morning I received devastating news. A Care worker from the unit came to tell me that Sian had been taken to the Psychiatric ward of a hospital in Epsom. I had thought that she was quieter than usual in class over the past few weeks, but on questioning she said that she was fine. I didn't manage to find out exactly what had led to this decision for her hospitalisation, in spite of my questioning. I was told that she had become out of control and staff had been worried for her safety. No more was said but I asked if Sian would like a visit from me, and the Care worker promised to let me know. I heard later that day that Sian would like me to visit, so arrangements were made that I would visit her on the following Saturday afternoon.

Saturday afternoon arrived. My husband had agreed to accompany me to the hospital. I knew Sian would not mind as she had met him on a number of occasions.

We set off with me feeling much apprehension. As we journeyed through the Surrey countryside I tried to relax. 'Would I say the right things? Would I be able to comfort her?' I kept asking myself. We arrived at the hospital and were directed to the Psychiatric wing. It was a pleasant enough place with flower beds and trees around. She had been given a private room, and on arrival was waiting for us. Going forward with a smile I gave her the small gift I had brought. She smiled but did not say anything. Any awkwardness was covered by my saying brightly. "Hope you don't mind me bringing my other half, but with my driving and sense of map reading, I didn't think I would ever get here.'

I looked around the room. It was quite bare, white walls with just the basic necessities such as a bed and a chest of drawers. There was no evidence that Sian had any personal possessions, except for a box of tissues, and other bits and pieces. "You can bring him if you want," she said.

Thinking to myself that I must lighten the atmosphere I asked her how she was. With such a disturbed child as Sian was, I had to tread carefully. "Sut wyt ti?" I asked her again, in Welsh this time, thinking it would break the ice. There was no place for visitors to sit down, as obviously visitors were not common in this part of the hospital. She did begin to relax. "Thanks for coming," she said "I'm ol right I s'pose, they said I got to be here anyway."

We chatted about school and I tried to make what I

said interesting, but it was very difficult. My heart went out to her, as she was obviously in distress. I put my hand out to her to try and bring some comfort, and she took it willingly. After the departure of the Sisters, the Welsh lessons had not been resumed. She must have missed these lessons but I knew better than to ask. I wanted to know how long she would be in hospital, but did not want to upset her by asking.

After about fifteen minutes, a nurse appeared, and from her body language I took this to mean our dismissal! Sian whose expression had not really changed the whole time, gave me a hug and said a brief goodbye. We were directed out of the building. The nurse was not unfriendly but had a tight-lipped attitude that forbade any possibility of questioning about her patient. I left the hospital feeling very low and asking myself 'What can I possibly do to help Sian?' I knew this question was futile as her future was not in my hands.

School was not the calm settled place it had once been. We were managing to keep discipline in classes, but I was noticing that many of the girls were developing a careless attitude towards what was going on. Whereas morning Assembly had been a looked- forward to good start to the day, it was fast becoming a non-event, with the noticeable absence of Care staff, and girls turning up late, looking as if they had not had a proper wash. I asked myself what was going on? I felt worried for them. Behavioural boundaries seemed to have disappeared. This couldn't-care-less attitude was more difficult to take than any overt bad behaviour was. Veronica just carried on with Assembly, giving out any notices or other matters to be dealt with, before dismissing us to our classes. Classes were smaller now as Local Authorities were not referring many girls. Most of the girls still wanted to work and carried out the tasks allotted to them. They liked the idea of being able to use a Computer, so were prepared to have a go.

It was a bleak morning, quite uneventful. I was pleased to see lunchtime, and was looking forward to chatting with the teachers, and catching up on all their news. Crossing the floor to the door of my classroom, I noticed with surprise that it was shut. It was a heavy oak door, difficult to close, and the girls always left it open. I tried to open it, and found that it had stuck. I found it difficult to believe, but it had been locked. The heavy brass key which was always left in the lock for the past seven years had been turned! I was locked in! I was surprised to find that although my first reaction should have been anger, I found myself seeing the funny side.

I opened the large window and looked down at the ground. We were at ground level, but the large Gothic style window was still quite high up from the lawn below. I looked at the windowsill, and seeing that it was very wide and would certainly hold my weight, I decided to take a chance, and as that was my only way of escape, I made my decision. I was very fit in those days so I climbed out, and jumped to the ground. Making my way back into the building towards the staffroom,

I saw a cluster of four girls sniggering in the shadows. I smiled at them, removed the key from the outside of my classroom door, and moved on. The teachers thought it was a huge joke, as they could see that I was not in the least upset, but I could see they were sympathetic towards me for what had happened.

"It's a good thing it wasn't me," said Janet. "I wouldn't have been able to climb out of the window." The girls concerned were very young and new to Ravenscourt. I did wonder, 'why me?' but consoled myself with the fact that I was the only one with a door containing a key! During the old regime a Community meeting would probably have been held to thrash out the matter, but as there was no such provision to deal with misdemeanours I decided to say nothing about it officially.

The following week brought good news about Stacy. Returning to school after half-term I was greeted with the news that she had left school, and was in a 'Holding Children's Home' in Surrey, which catered for teenagers on a short term basis, while they waited for a further placement, a flat or a return home.

Unexpectedly, Stacy's mum wanted her home on a set date in two weeks' time. I wondered why she had to move from Ravenscourt for just two weeks, but never found out. I was pleased to hear that she would like me to visit her with her Social worker. I thought to myself, 'oh no', I really didn't have the time to spare to go all that way into deepest Surrey. It was a busy time at the Drugline at the moment. As well as telephone counselling once a week, plus one evening face-to-face, I had taken on further voluntary work with them. I had started a Tranquilliser Support group for women who were finding difficulty with prescribed drugs. But I could not let Stacy down, so I readily agreed to the visit.

We arrived at the Home to find Stacy in good spirits. The place was most impressive. It was a large manor house in splendid grounds. Teenagers of both sexes were wandering around enjoying the gardens. Everyone looked happy with expectations that the future would be rosy perhaps? Stacy was thrilled that at last Mum wanted her home. We chatted for about half an hour, then she appeared tired. She was obviously anxious about her future, even though it did seem promising. We were given a cup of tea by a staff member and then took our leave. "You will come and visit me when I am at me Mum's won't you, Miss?" she said.

"Of course," I said. "Just let me know when," thinking as I said this that it would never happen, but surprisingly it did on a number of occasions.

Dana was still keeping in touch from time to time. She sent me a photo of herself with a group of friends, enjoying her 20th birthday party. She was enjoying life and still at college training for her Social work qualification. I felt very privileged when girls contacted me after they had left school.

One day after morning lessons, when I was clearing up, I was just about to go for a well-earned break, when a girl who had been in my last lesson, re-appeared through the door. "Hello, Fay, what can I do for you?" I asked. She was a new girl, and she had only been with us for a couple of weeks. Small in stature and very quiet, I knew that she was one of the abused children that so often arrived at Ravenscourt. These girls seem to handle the horrors of their backgrounds in different ways. Many appeared to rise above and not seem to care about the abuse they had suffered. Although this was just a front and their pain was almost as noticeable as it was in the girls who showed the pain in their faces. Dana had said to me on our very first meeting "You know, Miss, I put myself in Care. I just put all me stuff in a black plastic bag and that was that." I knew there must have been more to it than that, and I did find out later what the whole story was.

I brought myself back to the present and concentrated on Fay. "Out with it then, Fay" I said. "I'm dying for a cup of tea." I knew that whatever her problem was, she considered it to be important, so I waited patiently. I had been asked many questions by the girls and usually managed to come up with an answer, sometimes after discussion, so I felt I was quite prepared for it. How wrong could I be? I was certainly not prepared for this one.

"Miss, do you think I smell fishy?" she asked. I knew I had to come up with an answer, but I replied with a question. "Why do you ask that" I replied, playing for time. "Cos the girls say I smell fishy" she replied. She always looked clean and tidy, but obviously her personal hygiene left a lot to be desired, and I had not been close enough to her to notice. I wondered if she was being bullied by the other girls. I did the only thing I could do under the circumstances. We sat down together, and I gave her a little talk on feminine personal hygiene. She went away quite happy, so I felt that was another hurdle I had overcome. I felt that it was very brave of Fay to tackle her problem in the way that she had, by sharing it and hoping to find a solution.

I had always admired these girls for their openness and honesty, coming out with what they had to say, good or bad, always managing to stay on the right side of rudeness.

A girl once said to me "Do you know why we like you, Miss?" I knew this question was rhetorical and so she did not expect a reply. I waited, "cos you're strict but kind," she said.

"Thank you," I said.

CHAPTER FIFTEEN

On one occasion I was wearing my new blue and white seersucker blouse. This cotton material had been around since 1907, but was making a comeback in the 1980s in the form of dresses, blouses, and even men's suits. The press reported an occasion when seersucker suits were worn by American men attending an event for Ronald Regan.

Taken from the Hindu word 'Sirsaka' the material did not need ironing. The wrinkled look was part of the charm, or so I thought. Walking through the corridor on my way to lessons, I was greeted in passing by one of the older girls who said "Ain't you ever heard of an iron, Miss?" I just smiled in reply, and walked on. I found it quite funny.

I entered the staffroom to find all the teachers busily munching away at their various lunches which consisted of sandwiches, salads, fruit etc. They all stopped chewing and looked up. "Where have you been?", "What's up?", and other comments. They could obviously see from my expression, that something had been happening. I hesitated. "You don't really want to know," I replied. "Yes we do," they chorused. I related the story hesitatingly. I knew from an unwritten law that my words would never be repeated outside the staffroom, so I was safe there! My story was greeted with hoots of muffled laughter. It was a matter to be taken seriously, but I did admit that there was a funny side, and I tucked into my sandwiches.

It was Tuesday morning again, the start of my week and after a busy weekend I was in my classroom preparing for the day ahead. I looked at my watch, and thought it about time I made my way to Assembly. This was something I had always looked forward to during happier times, as there had always been a word of encouragement to us all, and a Spiritual word from Sister Mary. The girls accompanied by members of the Care staff, had always been well turned out. Things were somewhat different now. Today I felt a kind of despair. On entering the room where Assembly took place I could see that things were far from happy. A few girls were missing, probably with no good excuse. There was no smoking today, but I was horrified to see that one of them was wrapped in a duvet. Valuable classroom time was often lost as girls returned to the unit to finish dressing. Classes that morning went quite well and we all looked forward to a visit to the local indoor swimming pool that afternoon.

The following week brought some unhappy news about Sian, as her Social Worker contacted me to say that she had been transferred to a Psychiatric hospital in Northampton. There were no satisfactory answers to my questions. "Why Northampton?", "How did Sian feel about it?" "Was there discussion with her beforehand?" I felt cheered up as the Social worker said that Sian had asked that I was to be informed about the move. I felt anxious; what could I possibly do to help, with her so far away. She had been transferred to a new Authority so all official contact would be lost. I had to put my thinking cap on, and come up with something, which later on I did.

During the past six years the tutoring setup had been successful. Taking a special interest in your tutees was good for the girls, as it involved 'special treats' like taking them out for a meal. Therefore it was with some shock that I was faced with the following statement from Veronica. "From now on I am taking you off the Tutor list, as you are only part-time." As I worked four out of five days a week, Monday being my only day off, I was affronted. Also I had given a lot of my time during out-of-school hours. I was just as committed as the teachers that worked for five days. But the thing that annoyed me the most was that the tutoring idea had been mine, taken from the sixth form college I had been teaching in previously. I explained all this to her, but she was not into listening. This decision had been given to me in an offhand casual way, in an unprofessional manner. As numbers were down at the moment, most of the teachers had only one or two tutees.

There was another shock to come for me. Michelle was my only tutee at the moment, and it seems that I was losing her. Veronica had decided to transfer her to the new Home Economics teacher. I protested further, but it was no good. "I'm in charge and it's my decision," she kept repeating, as she usually did on these occasions. There was nothing more to say, but I thought to myself, 'You haven't heard the last of this.' Later that day I made an appointment for a meeting with the Principal Mr Williams. He never had much to say when he did appear. Let's see what he had to say about this.

The meeting was scheduled for the following afternoon at 2pm. News travels fast, as at the end of the day Veronica confronted me. "I hear you have arranged for a meeting with the Principal tomorrow afternoon" she said. "I would like to be present if you don't mind? How did she hear so quickly? I asked myself. I had shared this information with the teachers, but none of them would have told her. The possibility was that the Principal himself would have told her, and also asked her what it was all about. "You are quite welcome to attend," I said.

I arrived at the Principal's door promptly at 2pm. I tapped lightly on the door, and entered on his command "Come in," he said in a loud voice. I entered the room to find that Veronica had already arrived. He stood up as I entered, and motioned me to a chair which I thought was strategically placed as to give the impression that I was being interviewed by the other two.

He began "I hear that you have a complaint at a decision of Veronica's? What's it all about?" I stated my case, emphasizing the fact that the tutoring idea had been mine from the beginning, and taken on by the then Head of Education. He said very little, but appeared to be listening intently. He then looked over at Veronica. "What do you have to say?" he asked. Surprise, surprise, she said just what she always did.

"I'm in charge, and I make the decisions." I was incensed, but what could I say? I stood up and faced her, saying in what I thought was a loud voice, but came over quiet but strong.

"You might be in charge, and make the decisions, but I don't have to agree with you if I think you are being unjust." The outcome of the meeting was that the Principal decided that I was to be re-instated as a tutor.

'One up to me,' I thought, but for some reason did not feel elated. 'What a waste of time this has been,' I thought, when I could have been putting my energies into something more constructive. Entering the staffroom at break I told the teachers the result of the meeting. They were pleased for me, and had fully supported me in this, agreeing that I had been badly treated. It was a shame that there always seemed to be a current of unrest coming from Veronica. She was always bringing out the moan that all the teachers were not for her.

On one occasion she brought into the Friday staff meeting, a drawing of a bridge, showing where she thought the teachers were, in support of her. Little stick figures with our names on. She went through it, showing the position she thought we were. Interestingly, the only stick figure that appeared 100% with her was the new Art teacher who had been chosen by her. The rest of us did not take much notice of it.

She had tried the tactic divide and rule but that did not work with us. We were too strong and established a group for this to have any effect. We knew we were doing a good job in school to the best of our ability. For the most part, the girls' behaviour in school was good. Discipline was practised in the classroom, as the girls knew what was expected of them and worked and behaved quite well. The small behavioural problems were handled in the class, and this worked. The girls were the only thing that mattered in this establishment. Veronica had the problem. She should pull herself together and concentrate on that fact. School must be a safe place for the girls.

At a dinner party at the weekend I was seated next to a friend of a friend I had not met before. As you do, we exchanged pleasantries. The food was extremely good, avocado with prawns to start, followed by duck à l'orange and strawberry meringue. We continued chatting, and I noticed that my husband was in deep conversation with her partner. Listening for a brief moment I heard the word Rugby cropping up. 'What else would it be?' I thought, especially as both men had been at Twickenham Rugby ground that afternoon, to watch London Welsh at play. The 'inevitable' cropped up in the conversation; "What do you do?" asked Sheila, for that was her name. I told her, asking in return "What do you do?" expecting her to say "I teach at the same school as June," our hostess for the evening. The food took second place as I pricked up my ears at her reply.

"I am a teacher in the Education Department of the Young Offenders Institute not too far from here."

"Sounds interesting," I replied. We went on to talk of other things, families, holidays etc. The evening came to an end, and we said our farewells. As a parting shot Sheila called out to me as she was going through the door, "Don't forget, if you ever want to change jobs, they are always looking for teachers at the Young Offenders place, especially ones with Computer skills." She continued, "The head of Education is very approachable, the telephone number is in the book."

"Okay," I said, "Thanks." Thinking to myself that the idea of leaving the Children's home had never occurred to me. Anyway I decided it was worth bearing in mind.

It was a Thursday, it was autumn and the nights were drawing in. The clocks had not been altered so there was quite a bit of daylight left, as school finished for the day at 3.30pm. I was tidying up my room, but planned to leave on time as I had a Drug Counselling session planned that evening at 7pm. I entered the Staffroom to say my Goodbyes in time to see Jo, a member of care staff rushing in from outside. She was in tears, what on earth could have happened? I thought. She cried out "All the car tyres have been let down." Jo had just taken delivery of a brand new car, so she was very upset. The rest of us went out to the place used by the staff to park our cars. Sure enough it looked as though all the tyres were flat. Far from being upset, I was jolly annoyed. What about my Counselling session? None of us had mobiles, it was the 80s after all. There was no way I could contact my Client, as the only number I had for her was her home number and that was in my address book at home. I approached my car which was at the far end of the line. To my amazement, my car tyres were still intact. I took a second look, and saw that they had been left alone. Checking with the others, I realized that mine were the only ones left intact. We looked at each other and decided that this had to be the work of the girls. I was puzzled, why had they left my tyres alone? Perhaps time had run out as my car was parked at the end of the line, or maybe, as I sometimes thought, jokingly to myself, the girls thought that because I was a Christian, that I had a hot line to God, and therefore they had to watch out? Meanwhile Janet, taking charge had summoned Jim the handyman/gardener, and he obligingly fetched his hand pump and got to work. I went on my way as I was in a hurry.

Next morning in the staffroom, we unofficially discussed the matter of the tyres, questioning "Which of the girls was it?" "All of them? Or only one or two?" and the big question was "Why?" The Sisters would have held a Community Meeting for all staff and girls, and the matter would have been thrashed out. I had never looked forward to these meetings, but had to agree that they served a useful purpose in the maintaining of discipline. There had always been a successful outcome as the culprit or culprits had been taken to task. There would be no Community meeting this time, as this sort of discipline was out of the question in the present regime. We never did find out who the culprits were. I don't believe that this sort of behaviour would have occurred under the regime of the Sisters.

A few days later, a feeling I had never before experienced during my time at Ravenscourt came over me. I did not want to go to work, and the thought of facing the girls did not appeal. The teachers all carried on as usual, giving of our best, but our unspoken thoughts were still on the letting down of the tyres experience, and why the girls felt the way they did about the staff. We must put it out of our minds, difficult though it was.

I was still thinking about the dinner party, and the possibility of a job at the Young Offenders Institute. I told myself that I needed a change. No harm in writing to the Head of Education at the Institute. Probably nothing would come of it anyway. I posted the letter, and put the idea out of my mind.

The following week to my great surprise I received a reply to my letter, inviting me for an interview at the

Institute the following week. I panicked! Supposing I was offered a job, what did I know about Borstal establishments? The following week was half-term so I was free with none of the Teaching staff needing to know anything about it.

CHAPTER SIXTEEN

The day of the interview arrived. It was with some trepidation that I travelled to the Offenders Institute. 'What am I doing?' I asked myself. 'As if I am not busy enough, without taking on something I know nothing about.' The journey took 45 minutes, and on arrival I saw that the car park was enormous. 'However will I find my car again?' I thought.

With some difficulty I found my way to the entrance to the building which I found quite threatening. I entered the small doorway which opened up into a larger entrance type room containing three men who I took to be policemen, but later realised they were prison officers. They were stood behind counters with glass fronts. They greeted me pleasantly, asking my name. I felt I was being sized up, but it was probably in my imagination. Yes, they were expecting me at 2pm and someone would be along to escort me to the Education Wing.

This someone arrived four minutes later. She was a pleasant woman, very business-like and introduced herself. "I am Sylvia, Personal Assistant to the Head of Education, Vera Strange." I was led through another door which led to an open area with a narrow concrete path about half a mile long, leading to an enormous building which seemed to go on for ever. We were let in through the entrance to be met by two prison officers wearing all the gear one would expect, chain belt, keys and a whistle. They both looked kind and friendly, quite large of stature and I could imagine them being quite different when the need arose. One of them said "I will accompany you to the Education Wing which is not far." Sylvia would have known the way I thought naively, not realising the safety element that was needed in an establishment such as this. We were led down a number of corridors with doors on each side. These I later found out were the cells occupied by the inmates.

We entered a small room which contained a desk and a few comfortable armchairs. Vera Strange came out from behind the desk as I entered. She motioned me to one of the chairs and sat companionably in the other. She was quite a large woman with a friendly face and a quiet manner. The Interview felt more like a friendly chat than a formal meeting. I had already been sent an application form which I had filled in and returned. She knew my Academic credentials, but seemed more interested in my present work with teenage girls, my experience in Youth Work and more importantly my experience in the

Drug field. I was offered a cup of tea which I accepted gratefully. I was offered the job, to begin as soon as possible. I explained as it was only half-term I would be unable to give notice in my present position in time to begin the following term. Vera was quite happy to compromise for the time being. I agreed to start work the beginning of the next term, working only on a Monday, as that was my one day off, increasing my days when I was available. She seemed happy with this arrangement, so we shook hands, and Sylvia re-appeared and escorted me back the way we came. I thought it strange that we had not encountered any of the 'inmates,' but of course they had been in "lockdown" during the day. I drove home with mixed emotions, asking myself 'Was I doing the right thing?'

I had no time to spend questioning what I had done, as the following day we received an unexpected invitation to visit our daughter and family in Birmingham. We were now the proud grandparents of three lovely children. Two grandsons now, as our daughter-in-law had given birth to a baby boy, and our daughter had given birth to a baby girl. We were hoping to see them all as much as possible, so this was a very welcome invitation. My mind was working overtime. In my time away from school matters, I often thought of the girls and pondered on their 'doings'. I asked myself, was it possible that on our visit to Birmingham, we could call in to see Sian? Northampton was halfway between our Surrey home and Birmingham. I talked it over with my husband who readily agreed. I set out to make arrangements. It didn't seem right to just turn up, and a letter might not arrive in time. I decided to ring Sian's previous Social Worker. She would be able to put me on the right path. I obtained the telephone number of the hospital and was assured that Sian would welcome a visit from us. An arrangement was made for us to arrive early afternoon on the Thursday.

Thursday was a fine day and the journey to Northampton was without incident. My husband had mapped out the way to the hospital, so it was all straightforward. My only concern was what I was going to say to Sian? She was a bright girl and would certainly spot from my body language if I showed any pity. I must show encouragement and support as much as possible, difficult though it was. My mind was full of the ordeals that this child had gone through when she was very young, and still affecting her in her teens, and would probably affect her for the rest of her life. Hopefully everything would turn out alright for her in the end, if she received the right help and support. I pulled myself together.

It was a sunny day, I must concentrate on the weather. We drove into the hospital grounds full of mature trees and shrubs. The building did not look threatening so that was a comfort. We found our way to the Reception area and introduced ourselves. "Sian is looking forward to seeing you very much," we were told. A uniformed nurse led us down a couple of corridors which led to a section which appeared to contain small self-contained units. The nurse knocked on one of the doors and a small voice called "Come in." Sian opened the door, looking much smaller than I remembered her, had she lost weight, or was the vastness of the building affecting how I perceived her. She smiled, "Thank you for coming," she said. "Welcome to my little room." It was a cosy bed-sitting room, with a divan bed in one corner, two comfortable small armchairs set at a coffee table, with two straight-backed chairs set nearby. She motioned us to sit down. Sian's manners had always been impeccable and she had not changed. "I'm sorry I can't offer you tea as there isn't any," she said. We assured her that tea was not necessary. "Nice that you both could come," she said, looking shyly at my husband.

I had brought her a couple of small gifts. Some pretty handkerchiefs and a tin of talcum powder with a lily-of-the-valley perfume that I knew she liked. She thanked me and we spent some time talking about matters relating to personal items. I had been waiting for a break in the conversation to find out as much as I could about her situation. "How are you?" I asked. Thinking to myself what a silly question to ask, I moved on. "You are looking well." She was indeed looking her best as she had obviously made an effort. She was wearing a pretty floral dress in a variety of pink colours, with a matching pink cardigan. "You are looking very pretty," I added. She looked pleased. "It looks very nice here and the nurses are friendly," I said, hoping to get some information without it being too obvious I was asking.

"They told me I had to come here for my safety or something. So I just had to come. It's alright here. I've now got a new Social worker 'cos I'm in a new Council area or something." She did not seem to know what plans were for her future, unless she did not want to talk about it. "These people are doing stuff for me," she explained. Then looking directly at me she said in what was a loud voice for her "Who Cares." Was this a question, did she expect an answer, I was puzzled. Then before I had a chance to say anything, she turned the conversation away from personal matters. "How is school? I suppose in a way I miss it." She turned directly to my husband, as if she wanted to feel on safer ground, and not talk any more about her personal position. "How is your work?" she asked him.

The next ten minutes were spent in light mood as he related some of the antics and situations he faced in everyday life. She was interested and he managed to get her to laugh out loud, for which I felt grateful. Our time was soon up. It appeared that Sian had a certain amount of independence, but there was always someone on hand if and when needed. The nurse knocked and put her head around the door. "Are you finished?" she asked. "Sian has an appointment at 4pm. and she has to get ready." We said our goodbyes. I asked her to keep in touch and let me know how she was getting on, but I knew it would be difficult for her. A new Governing Board, and a new Social Worker, it would be impossible to keep track of her if she did not keep in contact with me herself. As we left I noticed that she was looking tired. I questioned the nurse on our way out, asking for any information she could give me as to what was going on. I told her that I was very fond of Sian, having taught her for a few years. I was told kindly, but in no uncertain terms, that as I was only her teacher, I had no right to know anything. This I understood, but she did fill me in with a few details. Sian had a certain amount of independence, but was unobtrusively watched due to her past efforts, if that's what they were to take her own life. She was encouraged to attend gatherings for learning purposes, such as craft or needlework, but part of her day was always given to psychiatric assessments and discussions on medication etc. According to the nurse it was one of these assessments that were taking place that afternoon at 4pm. She dismissed us in a friendly way as if to say she had given us all the information she was prepared to give. We took our leave. I felt rather unsettled as we continued our journey to Birmingham. I managed to switch off as I turned to other things, and concentrated on the pleasure it would be to see our two year old granddaughter again.

The second half of the term arrived. Averil was busy organising one of her very popular Saturday lunch gatherings for the girls who had left Ravenscourt. We all looked forward to these events. It was great to catch up with the girls, and a great many of them always turned up, sometimes alone, often proudly showing off their offspring, and occasionally accompanied by their husband or boyfriend.

Saturday of the lunch arrived, with members of staff arriving early to see what we could do to help, but the efficiency of Averil rendered us redundant in this area. She had prepared tureens of homemade soup with lots of chunky bread, plates of sandwiches, sausage rolls, crisps and other bits and pieces. The girls began arriving in what seemed to be droves. I was delighted to see a greater number than usual. Averil had a great knack of keeping in touch with them on a regular basis. There were quite a number of babies and toddlers, each young mum parading her offspring in a proud manner. I must admit I had never seen so many bonny babies. A great time was had by all as we caught up with the 'doings' of the girls. A number of them were holding down good jobs and were living in Social Housing flats. I'm sure they had the usual problems that life throws at us, don't we all, but I was so impressed by their maturity after the bad beginnings they had suffered. The lunch was held in the large hall at Ravenscourt with lots of room to move around and space for the children to play.

The highlight of my day was when Sandra, who with her beautiful baby son, and looking a picture herself, drew me quietly aside. "I've become a Christian, Miss. I thought you'd like to know." I was thrilled as she seemed so sincere. She could sense my delight as all I could say was "Well done," and give her a hug. She had really got it together. Averil and I had visited her six months before, where she was living in a purpose-built 2 bedroom Social Housing flat in a leafy Surrey suburb. I had been very impressed at her standard of housekeeping and baby caring. She had been working in an office for a couple of years before having her baby, and she told me that she fully intended returning to work as soon as he was old enough for Nursery school. She then told me the story of how she had unexpectedly met up with a group of friends who had invited her to their Church. It seemed she had been adopted by their family members, taken into their homes, and had even been provided with baby sitters on the odd occasion, as the Mums of her friends stepped in to help. I was further thrilled by an invitation to attend her Baptism which was to take place on the following Saturday in the local Secondary School swimming pool. Averil had already received her invitation so we could go together. I was excited and so looking forward to the following week. Time to leave came too quickly and we all said our goodbyes, hoping to see each other soon. As usual a great time was had by all.

Saturday arrived and Averil arrived to pick me up so that we could travel together, the 30 or so miles to the Secondary School in Surrey. We could not hide our excitement and chatted about what it meant for Sandra to be taking the big step involved in Baptism. Full immersion in the pool was a decision not to be taken lightly. She had received a lot of help from members of the church in teaching and supporting her through this

Spiritual journey, but she had also been blessed in ways that it is sometimes difficult for others to comprehend.

We arrived at the school and saw that it was a fairly new Comprehensive, comprising of a large low building with lots of plate glass windows. There were a few people milling about, mainly young. They smiled at us and we smiled back. They seemed quite excited. "Do you know the way to the pool?" they asked us. "It's our school so we know the way, and we could take you if you like?" After what seemed quite a long way, we arrived at the pool.

Most people were already seated in the viewing area, about 60 altogether, consisting of all ages with some quite young children. They all knew each other as they were members of the Church. They were a friendly lot and motioned us to seats. There was no sign of Sandra, but we knew she would be in an anti- room, getting ready. There would be a final preparation as the Pastor and his assistant would be saying prayers for her, and perhaps encouraging her to say a small prayer herself. There was a portable keyboard in the room and the pianist, who had been playing Spiritual songs very quietly, suddenly struck up a loud chord. It struck me that it was just like a Church wedding when the organist played to announce the appearance of the bride.

It was a large pool and the water would have been comfortably warm. The baptism would take place at the shallow end. The pastor appeared accompanied by a young man who was the Junior Pastor. They were both dressed in a white shirt and black trousers, as Baptist Ministers do not wear robes. They entered the water saying a prayer, consisting of what Sandra was about to do and uttering many blessings on the decision. Sandra now appeared dressed in a long white robe and looking very angelic with her long hair hanging loosely. We knew from our own experience that the robe was weighted around the hem so there was no danger of it floating up as she entered the water. She was accompanied by a woman who was carrying a large white fluffy bath towel. We later found out that she was called Jill and was a Deaconess at the Church. We could see that she was giving Spiritual as well as physical help to Sandra as she held her arm. The next words came as the Pastor, speaking directly to Sandra said how she had come to this decision and wanted to be baptised. Then came the familiar words, "Come and be baptised." It was a very moving service as Sandra, firmly held by the Pastors was immersed in the water three times. "In the name of the Father, In the name of the Son, and In the Name of the Holy Spirit," chanted the Pastor. Sandra came up, dripping wet, with a wonderful smile which seemed to hold a secret, that perhaps she would not share, as it was so special. She was then enveloped in the vast white towel, and led away. It was all over, and there was hardly a dry eye in the place, even among the men.

The members had set out a splendid tea in one of the rooms. Sandwiches of various kinds, salmon and cucumber, cheese and chutney, a salad, and a good supply of homemade cakes. Finally Sandra appeared, dressed in a blue dress, looking very serene and happy. Noah, her little boy was handed to her and she looked complete. He had been cared for by a friend as he played in another room. Sandra had to suffer hugs from everyone but she bore this gratefully. Averil and I were so pleased that she was so well and happy after all she had been through in the past. Every one of the girls who were or had been at Ravenscourt had suffered mental, physical, and/or sexual abuse in the past. I doubt if they would ever forget but if life was good to them they could move on. The afternoon came to an end and everyone agreed it had been a wonderful time and we were all blessed by the event. Averil and I sang hymns on the way home.

CHAPTER SEVENTEEN

The following week brought a drama we could all have done without. I arrived in the staffroom to find that all the other teachers had arrived, and for some reason they were looking very sombre. What could have happened? Had somebody died? I asked myself. It couldn't be that bad or I would have been telephoned at home. I was then faced with the terrible truth. A member of Care Staff had been found in bed with one of the girls. Jeremy was a comparatively new member of staff, having only arrived about 18 months ago. In his late twenties he had previously worked in a children's home in another country, where as we found out later, he had been accused of sexual demeanours, but whether or not he had been prosecuted we were never able to find out. Everyone working with children or young people had to have a police check, so surely it would have been picked up?

He was of course sacked on the spot. The girl concerned was very young, only 15 years old, and new to Ravenscourt. She was immediately sent off to a Secure Unit for her own protection and for the help she obviously needed. We all felt very upset for the young girl whose name was Daisy, and the conversation was very muted after that.

Looking back now, it seems unbelievable that this story didn't make it into the newspapers. But this was the 80s and things were very different in those days. There was not nearly as much Media interference as there is today. Also the staff at Ravenscourt were very dedicated and loyal, and never telling any of the 'happenings' of the time. It would have been easy to repeat these as 'dinner party fodder', but it just did not happen. We were all bound by an unwritten law "What happens between these walls etc.

Veronica was planning the end of term Teacher's meeting. To my great surprise she took me aside and asked "Do you think your friend with the swimming pool would let us have our meeting in her garden?" She had heard favourable reports from the girls, who enthused greatly about the garden and pool, and were always ready for another visit, especially as we were always made very welcome. Whether this request would be made welcome remained to be seen. I said I would ask, thinking privately that the request was a bit of a cheek.

On Sunday after church, I approached Sheena

tentatively. I made sure to put over that the request came from my Head of Education and that the idea was not mine. The reply came without hesitation. "Yes, that will be fine, just let me know the day and I can make sure that everything will be ready for you." (The changing rooms and shower unit building that overlooked the pool was normally locked when not in use). "There will be six of us, I said. During my first visit with the girls she had left us to it, but after providing hospitality and the great cake after the swim, Sheena had gained the trust of the girls who had asked where she was, and would she be joining us? I never joined in the swimming, and on future visits she and I would sit together chatting as we kept an eye on the proceedings.

The last week of term arrived, and on the Wednesday as planned, we arrived at Sheena's. I could see that Veronica was impressed by the sheer size and position of the garden, which was two and a half acres in all. I was pleased to see that she had bought a large bunch of flowers to give to our hostess. "Just as a thank you," she said as she saw me looking at the bouquet. We went up to the front door to announce our arrival and to present the flowers. Sheena smiled with pleasure. "How kind," she protested. "There was really no need." We explained that we had brought sandwiches and rugs to sit on the grass. Veronica had decided that no chairs and tables would be necessary, much to our dismay, but 'She was the Head and it was her decision.'

We unpacked our bags, settled on the grass and ate

our sandwiches. I noticed that Veronica had brought a rolled up towel which I guessed rightly, contained a swimsuit. As far as the rest of us knew, swimming had not been on the Agenda.

After lunch we got down to the business of the day. It was rather a sketchy meeting when nothing of real importance was discussed. There was no reference to any great forward planning. Alarm bells started to ring, and I thought to myself 'are things really that bad' immediately dismissing the thought. At the conclusion of the meeting, under the unspoken guidance of 'Our Leader' we moved to the chairs around the pool. The water sparkled under the hot sun and we all started to feel relaxed. This was great. It was as though we were in the middle of the countryside, and not in the middle of the London suburbs.

Our conversation turned to the forthcoming holidays. How much we were looking forward to the break, and what we had each planned to do. All of a sudden Veronica announced "I'm going for a swim, anyone coming?"

"I didn't know swimming was on the agenda?" piped up Janet.

The reply was "What's the point of coming to a swimming pool if we aren't going to swim?" Without further ado she disappeared into the changing rooms. She reappeared some minutes later, knowing that we were all looking at her. She had a good figure and the swimsuit looked very fetching, mostly black with silver bits strategically placed. As part of the act she walked swiftly over to the deep end and dived seamlessly in. The rest of us were impressed, but quickly lost interest as she swam up and down showing off her various strokes.

The sun was hot and we dozed in the shade under the trees that were dotted around. It made me think of the times when visiting Sheena's on my own on a social visit, I had seen her with this enormous net, fishing out leaves from the pool, especially in the autumn. Sheena was a keen swimmer and as the pool was heated, she swam every day, except in mid-winter.

All of a sudden I was alerted by a funny movement coming from the pool. 'What on earth is she doing?' I asked myself. Blinking and removing my sunglasses I could see more clearly. She had removed her swimsuit and was casually placing it on the side of the pool, before continuing her leisurely strokes up and down. The others hadn't noticed, or perhaps they pretended not to see. I was angry and upset, but was determined not to show it, as if I had said anything, it could have so easily turned into a row. I felt that her behaviour was totally unacceptable, and that she was abusing the hospitality of my friend. But the thing that worried me the most was that I knew that Sheena's two teenage sons were home on holiday from boarding school, and they could easily be looking out of one of the bedroom windows, which not exactly overlooking the pool, definitely had a good view of it.

I watched as about ten minutes later, Veronica calmly

retrieved her swimsuit, and struggled to get it back on. Count your blessings I said to myself, she could so easily have got out of the pool naked, and walked across to the changing rooms. The rest of the afternoon went by as in a blur as far as I was concerned. We eventually packed up, went up to the house to say our goodbyes, before driving back to school. I stayed in the background as Veronica enthused to Sheena on how much we had enjoyed the afternoon. I called out "Thanks very much, Sheena, see you on Sunday."

"Okay, look forward to seeing you then," came the reply.

I did see Sheena accompanied by her husband and the two boys, on the following Sunday. I held my breath. During coffee time after morning service all was normal, as everyone chatted. The boys talked about the school term that had ended and other matters that teenage boys discuss. I watched them closely, making a point of engaging them in conversation about this and that. Nothing seemed amiss. I assured myself, rightly or wrongly, that they had been saved the 'vision' of the Head of Education swimming naked in their pool. One thing I did know, that never again would I be asking for the use of their garden for any school meeting.

CHAPTER EiGHTEEN

The end of the school year approached with no further major incident. Some of the girls had seemed restless, maybe worrying about the long summer holidays, asking themselves, "Where will I spend the holiday?" or "Who will want me?" or other problems that always affected these girls. My heart went out to them, but there was nothing I could do unless of course they confided in me about a particular worry, and even then there was little I could do, other than have a word with the member of Care staff responsible for that particular girl.

For the most part they worked fairly well in class, but they lacked the enthusiasm and purpose of previous groups.

Plans were in hand as the care staff worked hard to find a place for each girl to spend at least part of the time away from Ravenscourt. A few girls were spending a short time with their parent/s under strict supervision from their Social worker, others were being looked after by the foster family they had known previously, others by a Foster Carer perhaps unknown to them but one who had been carefully screened and checked prior to being taken on to carry out this most important role in the life of one of these children.

I had looked forward to the six week holiday away from a busy schedule. We spent three weeks touring France, also spending time with our family. Our two small grandsons came to stay for a week, and we had a great time taking them on picnics, swimming, and visits to a farm to see all the animals and other activities to keep small boys of 3 and 5 happy.

The holidays passed all too quickly. It was time to get prepared for the new term. It was with some nervousness that I planned what I would do for my new Monday job at the Young Offenders Institute. I was employed to teach them an introduction to the Computer, Word Processing, and later on when I increased my hours to maybe include Office Practice, Bookkeeping etc.

Monday morning arrived and I set off early. The journey was a longer one than I was used to, taking the best part of an hour, negotiating traffic lights and busy roads at peak time in the morning. I switched the radio on, perhaps that would help me to relax.

I entered the enormous car park as I had done previously. I parked in a position I thought would be fairly accessible when I returned to the car later in the day. I walked to the first entrance. The brass handle on the large heavy oak doors turned with the minimum of pressure. I was in! The entrance room looked as before, two Prison Officers behind glass, looking very busy, but chatting to each other as they sorted out the beginning of their day. The difference this time was that they welcomed me with a friendly smile, as one of them said,

"Good morning, we've been expecting you. Do you know the way to the Education block, or shall I phone for someone to take you?" I assured him that I did know the way. The outer door to this entry room was unlocked and I stepped out, taking the path I knew would lead me to my destination. I arrived at the main entrance to the prison, to be met at the locked glass door by a further Prison Officer who I could see was expecting me. He unlocked the door with a key taken from the enormous bunch around his waist.

I tried not to make it too obvious as I looked at the bunch. I could see a number of large keys, a few small ones and several unidentifiable bits. Perhaps I would find out later what they were, although I recognised a whistle and what looked like a truncheon. I followed him down the same corridors as I had on the previous occasion, and he chatted about the weather amongst other things. I think perhaps he sensed my nervousness and was trying to put me at my ease, as we made our way past the rows of closed doors on each side.

This time one of them was open, with a Prison officer just standing inside. I could see into the interior which consisted of a small, but compact single room containing a bed, bookshelves holding a number of books and also there was a wash hand basin. There was no sign of the occupant, but maybe he was hiding behind the door. We walked on and arrived at the Education Area. I thanked the officer for accompanying me, he moved away, and I was alone!

The room was quite small, but comfortably furnished. As my classes started later, the rest of the staff would already be in class. There were dirty coffee cups on the table – evidence of people leaving in a hurry I thought. I sat stiffly on one of the empty chairs. No sign of life anywhere. The corridor I had been led down was seemingly quiet, but I was now aware of quite a lot of noise further away in the distance. I flicked through a couple of brochures that were lying around. After what seemed like hours, in fact as I glanced at my watch I saw that it had only been five minutes, the door opened to admit who I took to be an in charge person. From her body language it was obvious that she was a person not to be trifled with. She introduced herself and said "Sorry to keep you waiting. Welcome, we are so pleased that you have decided to join us."

She then reached into a capacious cupboard where there were rows of key belts hanging. With a smile she handed me one, saying "this is the necessary equipment." I looked down at the equipment which consisted of strong chain belt very similar to the ones I had seen the Prison Officers wearing with numerous keys and a whistle attached to it. I noted with relief, the absence of a truncheon! She helped me to fasten the belt, and probably to lighten the situation she said, "I thought that the belt I had chosen would be a good fit, that was clever of me." As we had not met before, I thought this statement a big odd.

She moved to a small ante room and I followed instinctively, thinking that this was the natural progression to the scenario, even though she had not indicated to me to follow her. She then moved to a corner of the room and pointed to a row of pigeon holes, one of which I was gratified to see had my name on it. This comforted me somewhat and made me feel part of the establishment. I was shown a reporting book with the firm instructions that at no cost should I ever fail to make full use of this important aid which had to be written in after each teaching session, and returned to the locked cupboard after use. This took me aback. 'What possible comments could I make?' I asked myself. Little did I realise in my naivety, that there would be much I would write as I unloaded the day's happenings and saw them in print. 'Were there any prizes for the tutor with the least or the most comments?' I mused on this question as I realised that the Boss, as I thought of her was speaking again. "That's all you need to know for now. The rest you will pick up. Have a coffee." She pointed in the direction of what appeared to be kitchens. "As your classes don't start until 11 o'clock, you have plenty of time."

On entering the kitchen I was surprised to see

a young man at the sink. He looked no more than a boy. I smiled brightly; "Hello," I said. I started to feel a bit more relaxed as I felt I was moving more into my comfort zone. My vast experience of young people had made me feel quite comfortable with them. He moved away from the sink. "Good morning," he said "and what can I do you for, tea, coffee, or something stronger, only the something stronger is off the menu today?"

I laughed saying "Tea is fine with me, it's too early for the something stronger anyway." He kept up an endless chatter, as he made my cup of tea, bowing over it as he handed it to me. Maybe he had inspirations to be a waiter. I judged him to be about 16 or 17. He appeared cocky and self-assured, as he worked hard to disguise the fact that he was probably a confused lonely lad who was being punished for what he might have considered to be a minor offence!

"I have been a good boy," he said, keeping up his jokey manner, "so I have earned privileges, and one of them is that I can work in the staff kitchen. Lucky me, enjoy your tea, there's nothing nasty in it." He was testing me out, as he watched my face intently.

We were interrupted as all of a sudden there was a loud buzzing coming from every area of the large Education block. "See ya," he called out as he moved away and I made my way back to the Staffroom. On entering I saw that there were now five new occupants. The buzzing had signalled that lessons were over and it was break time. 'Another hurdle to overcome,' I thought as I looked at the circle of chatting individuals, mainly female. Introductions were made all round and I was made to feel welcome thinking to myself that these people projected a more relaxed cheerful attitude than I had expected to find here.

The austere exterior of the place, the unlocking of three sets of doors and the checking and rechecking of my credentials which included a photograph, hardly made for a relaxing casual start to the day. As I had initially made my way along the lonely paths to the Education block I had been aware of the calls and whistles from behind the open barred windows of the cells. I didn't kid myself that the whistles were for me, as I guessed that these lads would whistle at a duck walking along, in order to cause a bit of a diversion.

I brought myself back to the present as I heard a male voice calling out "What are you doing here?" as another tutor appeared.

"The same as you I imagine," I quipped, as I recognised Nigel. We had met previously on a Course that we had both attended. I had no idea that he now worked at the prison as a Maths tutor. He appeared to be a popular member of the staff as he joked his way through the coffee break. I felt accepted as if the attitude of the staff was if you're a friend of Nigel's you're a friend of ours. This I'm sure was pure imagination on my part, but it brought me comfort.

After the break I entered what was to be an entirely new experience in my life. I approached the rack of files and picked up the relevant Register for the class I was due to teach. Taking a deep breath I left the comparative quietness of the Staff room and following the rest of the tutors we approached the area containing the classrooms. On opening the double doors I entered what was like another world. I had seen the inside of prisons on the Television in such series as Porridge, so I should have been better prepared. However I took it all in my stride. I encountered a huge room with several open staircases. There were rooms presumably classrooms on the ground floor, and above an open balcony consisting of rows of further rooms. As everything was made of iron, the noise was intense with the clattering of feet and chatter as Prison Officers led groups of boys into their classrooms.

My classroom was number 11 and was situated facing the top of the stairs. I made my way towards it and opened the door tentatively, the large room was empty. I was relieved as I was able to find my way around before my pupils arrived. The first thing I noticed on entering was a large push bell in the wall. I can see it to this day. A huge brown bell push surrounded by a white 'blob'. This couldn't be missed if I was in a hurry to press it in an emergency.

Luckily, I never had an occasion to use it. But I did not know that at the time. Moving into the room I saw a large cupboard which contained Text books, writing materials, pens and pencils, printing paper etc. In fact everything I would need to run my class successfully. The room was set out as the usual classroom, with desks and chairs, and contained eight P.C's which I was pleased about. Large barred windows looked out onto forecourts with pleasant flower borders. This was a good start. I noticed that the noise from outside the room was considerably reduced.

The door opened to reveal my first pupils accompanied by a Prison Officer. He ushered them in. I had not met him before, but he had been primed as he introduced me by name.

There were eight boys all shapes and sizes and all looked very young, as indeed did the Officer, although he must have been in his thirties! He introduced the boys briefly, but before leaving he pointed out the bell situated behind the door. "There's the bell," he stated quite loudly I thought, as if I could possibly miss it. "Do not hesitate to use it if you need to." I was glad to see him leave as I wanted to waste no time, as I got to know the boys and settled each of them separately with a set piece of work.

Of course as I expected they were sizing me up as we went along. Three of them I was pleased to see seemed to want to work, and already had basic keyboard skills and were ready to learn. True to form they were not really interested in me as a person, but only how far they could push me in a quiet but talkative way. Each in their own way demanded a portion of my attention. They did not want me to remember their names but were keen for me to know what they were in prison for. "Do you know what I'm in for, Miss?" said Danny, a small cheeky looking lad.

"No why would I?" I replied. I was hoping in this first lesson to establish some ground rules. These lads were one of the two groups I would be teaching each Monday, using the same classroom each time so it should not be too difficult. I had decided to answer their questions if appropriate, so long as it did not interfere with the learning process. Unknown to them they were setting out some ground rules also. They needed to know where I stood in relation to maybe understanding where they were coming from. From time to time they threw words at me such as ABH, GBH, and street names for certain drugs to find out how street wise I was, if at all. I did not mind this, as it was all done politely and without malice. I fell in with this as I usually replied in words of one syllable.

Almost at the end of the lesson, when the boys were working away or otherwise deep in their own thoughts while looking around, an occurrence I could have done without happened. All of a sudden there was a sound of many whistles being blown outside, accompanied by the rushing of many pairs of feet running and much shouting. The boys instantly got up in unison and rushed to the window. I must admit that instinctively I went over to the window also, in time to see about 25 uniformed Prison Officers blowing whistles all rushing in one direction. Something was up and we were all captivated by the scene. They must have been used to it, but for me it was a totally new experience, only seen in films! Only a couple of minutes had passed, but it was time for me to take control. "Come on now boys, it's time to get back to work," I said, looking straight at them and using my most authoritative voice. They all obeyed and the rest of the lesson passed without incident. They were collected by the Officer and one or two actually said "thanks, Miss." I seemed to have passed muster, but it was early days yet!

There was so much negative publicity about Young Offenders Institutes, and very little positive sides, as if none existed. I was very impressed by the Education Department of this one. A range of subjects was taught, the boys having earned the privilege of attending classes by their good behaviour. It was lunch time and everyone had brought sandwiches as being an out of town establishment there was nowhere to get anything to eat.

After lunch a young woman in the group approached me. I had been introduced to her previously and recalled that her name was Ania. "I am the Art teacher," she said. "I was wondering if you would like to look around the Art room?" I thought that this was a very kind gesture and immediately agreed. She led the way through a couple of corridors and threw open a door at the end of one. The gesture seemed a bit dramatic but then I saw why. In front of me was a large room containing the usual paraphernalia of an Art room, but I was not prepared for the fine array of paintings covering the walls. She was obviously very proud of the achievements of the boys under her obvious talented teaching, hence the invitation. She looked at me and could see that I was impressed. I don't know a lot about Art but I sensed that one or two of these were very good.

I spent a little time looking at the pictures, and could see that in many of them the life experiences of the boys were portrayed. There was a picture of a child crying, and that probably meant something to the artist. There was 'subdued' fighting and abuse, as it wouldn't have done to use graphic images. I could have spent more time looking at this impressive work, but lunchtime was over and we had to get back to work. I expressed my desire to return on another day, and this I did.

My first day working at the prison came to an end. I summed it up as I proceeded to find my car. I felt it had gone well. Everyone had been kind and supportive and the boys had proved to be cooperative on the whole. I hoped I had shown them that I wouldn't put up with any nonsense. I returned home feeling quite satisfied with my day.

CHAPTER NINETEEN

Tuesday saw the beginning of the new term at Ravenscourt, and so life went on. I soon got used to the routine of including the Prison into my weekly teaching regime.

Life at Ravenscourt proceeded much as usual. Class sizes were diminished as Local Authorities were not making referrals on the same scale as previously. Morale in the Teachers' staffroom was not as high as before, but nothing was openly voiced. Was it fear of the future that kept us carrying on as though everything in the garden was rosy? We were all a little more subdued than before. As teachers we had become friends and it was the 'norm' to share our highs and lows. Why not now I asked myself? In spite of this we all remained cheerful and positive and encouraged the girls to work hard to achieve certain goals they had set themselves and so doing so help them to build their self-esteem and confidence.

My first term working at the Prison was coming to an end. I had a decision to make. I was enjoying teaching the boys in spite of the challenges I encountered which were nothing I could not handle. I never had to ring the bell for help. The job was not very rewarding as many of the boys were on Remand and only at the Prison for a short period, after which they were moved on to serve sentences as their future life unfolded before them.

I had made the decision I could not leave the girls. After eight years, part of me had become part of Ravenscourt and I would not go unless I was pushed. Also I could not leave the Teachers as I felt I would be leaving a sinking ship. Or was I being over-dramatic?

The Head of Education at the Prison was very sympathetic when I gave in my notice. She had fully understood my point of view about the situation, and assured me that should I wish to return at any time on a part-time basis, there would be a place for me. I was very touched, we parted on good terms and I left at the end of the second term.

The news came before the end of the year. Ravenscourt was to close. This was not totally unexpected. Our first concern as teachers was for the few girls that were left. We were assured that each girl would be found a place that would be suited to their particular needs. They had accepted the news. This was for them just another change in their young lives. We were of course upset for ourselves. We had spent eight years together as a small productive group of teachers. It was a shame it was to end like this. All the staff had to go all out to find jobs in quite a short time. We also worried about the financial aspect. Would we get redundancy pay? Janet, as capable as ever announced "I will get my Union rep. to come and talk to us. I'll get on to it right away." This she did and after negotiations were completed we were each awarded redundancy pay.

We all did our best to keep up morale until the leaving date. The girls were each found a place that was suited to their particular needs, and disappeared one by one with no ceremony. It appeared at the time that they were just 'whisked off'.

There was a lot of clearing up in the school premises. Books to be packed in boxes and furniture removed. It was all taking place by professional removal men, our help was not needed. The PC's were to be sent to an Education unit in a nearby town.

Averil was busy organizing a leaving BBQ for all staff during leaving week. We were looking forward to it, but on the other hand dreading it, as this would be our last day and we would be saying our farewells.

The weather was good on the day of the BBQ, and we all spread out over the vast lawn, taking out chairs and tables. We spent most of the time talking over the good times we had experienced together, and our hopes for the future. Many of the Care staff had obtained jobs and some had already left to take up their new post. Others were still job-seeking.

We seemed a light-hearted bunch as we laughed

and joked and shared our plans. The teachers had all obtained a job even though it was not exactly what they would have chosen if given the choice.

As for me, a return to mainstream education did not appeal, so until I decided where my future lay I had applied for and obtained a post as a Part-time Youth worker for the local Council.

The BBQ was over, the clearing up done, our goodbyes to the Care staff over, the Teaching staff said their goodbyes. There was sadness, but relief too that what had been a painful three years had finally come to an end. One or two were in tears, and the rest of us felt the emotion that saying goodbye after eight years of working together brings. We promised to keep in touch, and we did meet up from time to time.

The local Drugline service was expanding and I had been offered a job as Drugline Co-ordinator, on a voluntary basis. After quite a bit of hesitation I accepted, but I made it quite clear that this was to be on a temporary basis only. I thought that my work as a Youth Worker and my Voluntary work with the Drugline would keep me busy for the foreseeable future, but as it happens, my future did take on a completely new turn, quite unforeseen at the time.

Over 25 years ago I moved back to Wales, and to this day the teachers keep in touch with one another, even if it's only cards and letters at Christmastime.

ABOUT THE AUTHOR

Joyce Elizabeth Davies was born in Swansea, South Wales and moved to the London area after her marriage, where she worked as a Secondary and Further Education Teacher for a number of years.

Looking for a challenge, in the 1980s she obtained a post as a teacher in a CHE (Community Home with Education) caring for disturbed teenage girls who had suffered mental, physical and sexual abuse in varying degrees.

On returning to Wales she studied a Creative Writing Course for a couple of years, and with the help and encouragement of her Tutor, she decided to write an account of the eight years spent as a teacher at the Home.

Printed in Great Britain
by Amazon

18881108R00120